"This beautiful book is unlike anything else I have read. Toni shares her heart and her intimate relationship with Jesus in an amazingly vulnerable way. She walks the reader through her personal dialogues with Jesus, inviting us into difficult, messy interactions that eventually lead her to a place of joy. She draws the reader to be a part of this same process with thoughtful, probing questions that are full of grace and gentleness for the journey. If you are searching for a new way to grow in spiritual and emotional health, this book is for you!"

--Sandy Fitzpatrick, Occupational Therapist, California

"This book is exceptionally well-written and insightful. It is full of useful and penetrating application of scripture. Toni Daniels exhibits the truth that strength is found in vulnerability, and recovery is found in courage. She allows the reader to examine and reflect on the presence of Christ in their life by giving us a brave example in herself. Each chapter is fresh, well researched, engaging, and thoroughly honest. It is often honest in a way that can be scary at times. However, in being authentic and personal, Toni Daniels gives her reader the authority to be honest themselves."

--Kevin Compton, Tennessee

"Toni puts her life on display with a raw transparency that invites us to honestly examine our own lives. Her stories of discovering Jesus in the midst of her own self doubt, emotional pain, and nagging shame show us how the love and grace of God can transform us from the inside out. Her way is not the way of clichés or platitudes, but rather the hard work of honesty, authenticity and making space to truly listen to God. Toni's life and stories inspire me and challenge me to follow her example in my own faith journey. I highly recommend this book."

--Steve Adams, author of *Sacred Intersections*,
Director of Latin America for Comunitas International

"Transformational principles for intimacy with God and people, but, not just theory. Toni has lived this out, and in her book you see real life application of the principles with amazing vulnerability. We have recommended this book to all of the house church leaders in our Community.

--John White, Founder and Director of LK10 Community
(http://www.lk10.com/)

Back to Joy

*An Intimate Journey with Jesus into
Emotional Health and Maturity*

TONI M. DANIELS

Download the audio version of Back to Joy for FREE!

Simply go to http://back-to-joy-audio.launchrock.com/, enter your name and email and get access to the Free audio version of *Back to Joy*.

That's right! I would like to offer you the audio version for FREE as a gift for purchasing *Back to Joy: An Intimate Journey with Jesus into Emotional Health and Maturity*

DEDICATION

This book is dedicated to every person who has ever delighted in
me, and to all those in whom I delight!
This joy is the foundation on which I have built my life.
May we never underestimate the power of simply enjoying
each other!

Table of Contents

Acknowledgments 13

A Note to You, the Reader.. 15

A Little about Me 18

**PART I: Sporadic Moments with the Divine
(1982-2005)** 23

    CHAPTER 1: Beginnings.................................... 25

    CHAPTER 2: Returning to the Past to Free the Present . 30

    CHAPTER 3: The Gift of Difficult Relationships 39

    CHAPTER 4: The Power of Silence........................... 53

    CHAPTER 5: It Takes Time Sometimes.................... 64

PART II: Discovering Wholeness (2006-2010) 72

    CHAPTER 6: Intent versus Impact.......................... 74

    CHAPTER 7: Pride, It Finally Makes Sense........................... 87

    CHAPTER 8: I am Not a Powerless Victim........................... 97

    CHAPTER 9: Imaginative Play in Prayer 103

    CHAPTER 10: Perfect Peace Moves In.................... 109

**PART III: Walking With Immanuel (God with Us)
(2010-2012)** 114

    CHAPTER 11: God with Me: Physical Experience of
Spiritual Reality 117

    CHAPTER 12: God with *Us*: Confirmation that I am Not
Crazy 126

    CHAPTER 13: He is the Strong One 133

    CHAPTER 14: Becoming Free to Be Fully Me.................... 139

    CHAPTER 15: Let the Training Begin 147

PART IV: Learning to Receive (2012-2013) 155

    CHAPTER 16: My Needs are Valid 157

CHAPTER 17: With Joy Comes Grief 165

CHAPTER 18: Getting Back the Good 170

CHAPTER 19: Appreciation, God's Way Back to Joy 176

CHAPTER 20: Living into a New Reality 188

PART V: Learning to Suffer Well (2013-2114) 197

CHAPTER 21: The Man with the Sandwich 200

CHAPTER 22: The Man on the Bike 205

CHAPTER 23: Nothing is Beyond His Healing 210

CHAPTER 24: The Angry Eyes 216

PART VI: New Chapter (2014-2015) 223

CHAPTER 25: Becoming a Vibrant Family of Jesus 224

CHAPTER 26: Taking Ground 233

CHAPTER 27: Hope from Ashes 238

CHAPTER 28: A Few of the Gifts 246

PART VII: The Chrysalis (2015) 253

CHAPTER 29: For the Joy Set Before Me 255

CHAPTER 30: Not Alone 261

CHAPTER 31: Deeper Still 268

CHAPTER 32: *True* Self Space 273

A Word After 282

Appendix: Helpful Resources 285

ABOUT THE AUTHOR

Nicknamed "Sunshine" for the joy that she exudes, Toni Daniels has always loved being with people and creating spaces of belonging and meaning. At the early age of 16, after a short-term missions trip to Jamaica, Toni dedicated her life to serving abroad and sharing the hope of Jesus with those who would never otherwise hear about His great love. From leading worship and facilitating small groups throughout high school and college, she and her husband, Matt, moved to Uruguay, South America to start a church among the 'most unreached group of people in all of the Americas,' as described by Operation Mobilization.

After embedding in Uruguayan society, Toni and Matt quickly discerned that traditional church, as most know it, would never become a self-propagating movement in Uruguay. People would only come to faith in God as they could sense Him enjoying them in family and friendship settings. Driven by their desire to see Jesus lived out in real life, Toni and Matt began focusing on creating "healthy, vibrant families of Jesus" that would be able to transform the world around them.

Also drawn to provide emotionally safe places for children to explore their Christian spirituality, Toni introduced Godly Play (www.godlyplay.org) to Uruguay in 2006. To date, she has trained over 200 teachers and catechists, and more than 2,000 children have had the privilege of being a part of the community of Godly Play.

As an Interpersonal Relationship Specialist and Pastoral Counselor with more than 15 years of international experience offering training workshops and skills-based coaching, Toni's passion is to help establish joy-filled, Christ-Centered environments that produce healthy relationships and increase resilience.

Toni is currently the Director of The Geronimo Center for Innovation and Leadership (www.christianassociates.org/where/latin-america/geronimo-center), which she co-founded in 2008 with her husband, Matt. This Uruguay-based, non-profit organization seeks to initiate a revolution of joy in the most secular and suicidal nation in the Americas by forming emotionally healthy leaders from all sectors of society who follow Jesus in transforming their world.

Toni's undergraduate work focused on Spanish and Sociology. She also has a Master's in Leadership and Church Planting from Columbia International University. While in Uruguay, she completed her diploma in Psycho-Spiritual Counseling from the *Universidad Católica de Uruguay* in 2009. Other specialized training includes a certificate in Healthy Interpersonal Relationships from the International Trainer's Association and PREP, inc. (www.prepinc.com), a relationship enhancement training based in Denver, Colorado. She is currently working to finish the three-year Thrive Leadership Training with Life Model Works (www.lifemodelworks.org).

Toni's hobbies include karaoke, quilting, and sports. She loves being outdoors and spending time building joy with family and friends, especially her husband, their three children, and her poodle, Champagne.

To contact Toni about speaking engagements, retreats or training opportunities, or if you just want some free training videos and resources, visit www.tonimdaniels.com.

Back to Joy Resources for You!

Dear Joy-Journeyer,

These pages might just open wide the doors to a world full of joy. The deeper you go, the more joy you will grow. As with most work in life, "you get out of it what you put into it." Your soul will go even deeper when you take the risk of traveling with a few trusted others. Here are some resources I have included that may help you on your "back to joy" journey:

Personal Reflection Journal:

Journaling questions are included at the end of each chapter.

For a PDF version for printing and handwriting your answers go to www.tonimdaniels.com/wp-content/uploads/2016/04/Back-to-Joy-Journal-Questions-PDF-journal.pdf.

For a Form version for computer journaling go to www.tonimdaniels.com/wp-content/uploads/2016/04/Back-to-Joy-Journal-Questions-Word-Digital-Journal.docx.

Small Group Facilitator's Guide:

For a small group facilitator's video guide with questions for facilitating a small group discussion around the book go to www.tonimdaniels.com/video-blogs

Community Access and Resources:

We have also formed a Back to Joy Facebook group where you can connect with other "joy-journeyers," reflect together, and resource each other.

Know that my thoughts, prayers, and hopes are with you as you embark on your own "intimate journey into emotional health and maturity." And, more importantly, rest deeply in the fact that Jesus as "Immanuel," or "God with Us" is nearer than your next breath, and is holding you every step along the way.

Glad to be traveling with you during this season,

Acknowledgments

This book would never have happened without the help of the following individuals or groups:

Jesus, my Lord, my Savior, my Friend, my Father, and the Lover of my Soul. Not only did You make my story worth telling, but You also believed I could do it and convinced me to begin this work of remembrance. I would never have thought this possible.

My family, especially my Dad. Everyone's willingness to be vulnerable and exposed for the sake of the Gospel is inspiring. Going down memory lane has not always been fun. Thank you for leaning into the difficult places and letting grace cover a multitude of sins. Our closeness as a family is a treasured miracle of God!

The Beta Team. Stephen Johnson, Kara Moses, Tina Moore, Billie Brackeen, Taylor Garaguso, Steve Adams, Sandy Fitzpatrick, Susan Daniels, Marion Entz Harris. Your eyes were the first to get inside my internal world! You confirmed that I was not crazy, and that this book really could help people grasp what a relationship with Jesus looks like! I am indebted to your belief in me.

My editorial team, John White, John Shaw, Tammy Lancaster and my husband, Matt Daniels. You are the amazing team that has pushed me to be better than I could ever be on my own. Thank you for your insights, suggestions, and diligence in this endeavor.

My husband, Matt Daniels. Yes, you are in here twice☺ Thank you for formatting the book, setting up all of the systems and making this really happen. Without you these words would still just be a file on my computer! You have been my biggest fan. Thank you for creating the space for abundance to dwell.

Friends. Those of you from elementary school all the way to new friends, all really came through for me. Thank you for getting involved, joining the Launch team and encouraging and promoting this book in every way you have. It means so much to me to have you all on this mission together of inspiring others towards an integrated, Christ-centered, joy-filled life!

And lastly, the SPS Community. Thank you for giving me structure, accountability, coaching, and a really great blueprint to make this happen. And a special thanks to Angie Mroczka, my SPS coach. Thanks for being there.

A Note to You, the Reader

No matter where you are in life – whether you are just starting out, in the throes of building a career and raising a family, or encouraging and supporting an entire community – at every point, if you plan on being happy, you must have close, intimate relationships. And in order to have close, intimate relationships, you must learn to navigate difficult emotions well, even if those emotions belong to someone else.

Joy, that feeling you get when someone is glad to be with you, has the power to manage all that goes on inside of us... when there is enough of it. Unfortunately, however, for many of us there is very little joy inside compared to the shame, fear, sadness, anger, and hopeless despair that swirl about. The result of this imbalance is emotional shutdown or meltdown, which leave us unable to fully connect with those around us. Depression and addiction run rampant when joy is lacking. Yet most of us are never shown healthy ways to deal with our emotions, to express them well, or to build the joy we need in order to endure the hardships of life. This is precisely what I intend to do in the pages that unfold.

As a Pastoral Counselor, Cross Cultural Professional Minister, Relationship Coach, and Director of a fledging international leadership development center, my job is to make sure our leaders from all sectors of society have the joy and relational skills necessary to maturely handle whatever disaster or difficulty comes their way. After 18 years of working with leaders in Uruguay, one of the most depressed and suicidal nations in all of the Americas, I can tell you there is hope! We can grow joy, learn to quiet our minds, and build emotionally and spiritually healthy relationships that bring us great satisfaction and happiness.

In this book, I want to give you an intimate look into my back-to-joy journey. For most of us, knowing *what* we should do and *how* to do it is not enough. We need to see it in action. We need to see new options for how to handle old problems. We need to know the nitty-gritty of what these abstract concepts look like on the inside of a soul. This is why I invite you into my journey with Jesus toward healing and maturity by sharing with you selected private journal entries spanning these last 18 years.

The entries I have chosen to share are the moments when the Divine Himself intervened in my journey to bring a change in my heart and mind. You will find them in chronological order because I want to show you the progression my back-to-joy journey has taken and how each skill or resource has helped along the way. While reading in order will give you the bigger picture of how God has worked in my life, each story does stand on its own. Therefore, you can skip around if you are drawn to certain years or to a certain section. Follow your instincts and your heart.

My hope is that, through my story, you will see what it has looked like to struggle through my own emotional confusion and find my way back to joy. For me, it has not been a one-time event, but a lifelong process that has involved a relationship with the ONE who is an infinite source of "being glad to be with me," Immanuel, or God with us.

For those of you who struggle to manage your own emotions, may you know you are not alone. You are in good company. There are many of us out here who feel strongly, and we add excitement and flavor to the world. Our emotions are a gift, especially when managed well. I hope you find compassion for yourself and joy on the journey.

For those of you who do not feel much at all, or who manage to rarely feel overwhelmed, may this book help you understand those around you who seem to need a little more emotional support. I hope you find compassion for others and understand more fully how to enjoy them in life-giving relationship.

I am honored to be able to share my intimate, internal process with you. As you read, you may find that some of the vignettes are intense or even disturbing for you. I encourage you to stop and journal whenever you feel curious or sense memories, thoughts, or emotions stirring within. For this reason I have included personal reflection questions at the end of each chapter. This book is not meant to be read straight through. It would be best read a little each day, giving your soul time to ponder not only *what* you are reading, but also *how* you are responding to what you are reading. May your soul find the story it needs right now to move you into your growing edge and discover the Divine waiting there for you. Thank you for letting me be a part of your life in this small way. Let the journey begin!

A Little about Me

Whenever I get bogged down in emotional pain, crying my eyes out, I often wonder, "How do other people do it?" How do they deal with the intense pain of a broken relationship, a broken marriage, a broken child, broken dreams? How do so many people seem to get by without ever looking like they are hurting? Do they just push every pain so deep inside that they are unaware it is even there? Do they hide it with success and performance? Do they eat it away, drink it away, or escape it away? Or, do they just feel it and move on without losing a day of work? And if so, HOW!?

Then there are those who are unable to perform their way into feeling good; what do they do? Do they just limp through life feeling lost and less-than? Do they share their pain with others? Are they seen in their pain? Or do others avoid them because they are so uncomfortable with someone who can't seem to "get it together" that they have to run the other way, distance themselves, or blame the pain on the person?

And where am I on the spectrum? Do I go back and forth, one day feeling successful and strong, the next feeling lost and less-than? And so, the question becomes, "How do **I** do it? How do **I** handle intense emotional pain?" Because, in the end, I am the one who has to handle it for myself. There is no one else who can get into my skin and deal with **MY** pain...or is there?

I am still figuring all this out. While this journey encompasses almost half of my life, these last 6 years in particular have been incredibly fruitful, as I have come to train under an amazing group of psychologists, pastors, and coaches from Life Model Works, an organization that seeks to reintroduce missing relational brain skills into families, schools, and churches. Their goal is that these skills then become self-propagating within our communities, meaning that as we learn the skills we need to thrive in our relationships, we will naturally pass them on to those around us.

As a result, our communities will become safe places for people to mature and grow. Their movement, Joy Starts Here (www.joystartshere.com) has had an incredible impact on how I relate to those around me, as well as how I deal with the pain of difficult emotions. These mentors have taught me that joy is one of those brain skills that has been lost.

Joy is the feeling I get when someone is glad to be with me no matter what. It is the key to dealing with my strong emotions. Other factors include belonging to a community, having compassion for the weak, and somehow sensing the presence of the Divine with me, inside me. Immanuel, God with us, God with ME.

It has been said that Jesus did not die and come back again just so that we could go to heaven, but He died and rose again so that He could come to earth and accompany each one of us on this journey called life. Our journey is not about trying to get to heaven, but about living in relationship with our Creator now, here, so that a bit of heaven can be realized here on earth. Somehow, He wants to be our eternal source of "being glad to be with me no matter what." Somehow, He wants to be with us in our pain so that we can not only bear it, but also move *through* it toward a more mature self.

As a child, on a few occasions, I happened upon this "Presence" within. I am not sure why I could sense Him. Maybe it was because I had a wonderfully loving mother who built a strong base of trust in my brain, maybe I was more spiritually sensitive than others, or maybe that was simply characteristic of being "a child." Who knows? But I know this "listening" ability was not noticed, taught, or cultivated in my Christian community. Many believed that God did not speak to us outside the Bible, and therefore, we should *read* to hear Him, NOT look within where the Holy Spirit promises to be. They believed our imagination to be dangerous and fallen and not to be trusted. This was perhaps the most damaging false teaching I was ever taught by my precious, well-intended fellow believers.

So, as an adult, I was completely untrained in quieting myself and letting the Divine Creator speak to me through my imagination. I was a pretty successful church planter, missionary, and disciple maker, but after 16 years of being a Christian, I still ultimately felt alone, abandoned, and unloved. I desperately began a journey to follow God's presence inside of me, and specifically inside of my emotional pain. Quieting my mind, learning to discern my voice (versus God's voice, versus someone else's voice) has taken time. I have had to cultivate this ability and nurture it, always subjecting what I hear to Scripture and my community. But the journey has been more than worth it as it has led me to a wholeness where, even in my pain, I now feel hopeful, not alone, deeply enjoyed, and incredibly precious.

Following the Divine Presence into my emotional pain has led me at times to past memories. Going to the past is never easy. For some reason, we want only to remember the good about our childhood, our caregivers and our families of origin. It's almost like we think that if we acknowledge the painful, difficult, and unhealthy moments, we negate all of the beauty and health that was there. Or, we feel it might be disrespectful to our parents or other caregivers to share the ways we were unintentionally hurt by them. The complexity that we can love each other deeply and hurt each other deeply gets lost in the immature understanding that things are either all good or all bad.

The reality is, however, that we are both. We love deeply and we unintentionally hurt deeply. The fact that we cannot perfectly give our children *all* that they need, *all* the time, does not mean we do not love them with all of our hearts.

I know my parents have loved me with *all* of their hearts. When I look back to my childhood, there is so much good to remember. Music and sports created a tight family identity that we now enjoy with grandchildren and great-grandchildren. We sing karaoke and dance until all hours of the night. We know how to have fun together and it shows. We create belonging everywhere we go.

Most of my friends who know my parents have said that they only dream of having parents so engaged, so filled with sacrificial love, and so fun to be with. I appreciate the hard work we all have done to have the beautiful relationships that we have, because I know it has taken work on all of our parts. And I am so thankful for every good gift my parents have given me. I, indeed, belong to an amazing family.

Going to the past, however, has been necessary in order for me to become aware of the seemingly "not-so-good" gifts I got from my family of origin. These "gifts" did not seem like gifts for years, because unprocessed, they fester and are the breeding ground for contempt, bitterness, division, and isolation. And the saddest part is that if we do not go back and understand them, if we do not begin to own our story, then, our story will own us. These negative attitudes, shameful thoughts, or immature ways of seeing ourselves, others, or the world will be passed down to our own children.

On the other hand, when we follow Jesus back into our painful moments, He has the power to not only neutralize their damage in our lives, but to turn them into encounters with the Divine Creator who brings joy, peace, and healing.

So, I do not share these painful memories with you to air dirty laundry or make my family look bad. I share them with you in hopes that you will be able to see how little things can cause great damage; how wounds you thought were "nothing" might still be affecting your soul's ability to have healthy, intimate relationships; and how your present struggles, whether at work or at home, could be tied to your past unhealed wounds.

I also share in the hope that you might see how Jesus' touch can turn even an abusive situation into a joy-filled tender moment that gives you strength and purpose to live the present and to dream about the future.

It is precisely because of the "mistakes" my parents made unknowingly in raising me that I am who I am. Because of the particular ways I was wounded, I have a passion for creating safe places for children by developing emotionally healthy leaders who sense God's presence in their daily lives and in their communities. I am thankful that I was lead to look back, for it is out of my deepest pain I have found my greatest calling.

In what follows, I want to show you a different model for how to deal with the pain of living, loving, and losing in this broken world. Not a model that numbs it away or performs it away, but an example of walking through it with someone on the inside of you, someone who knows more about you than anyone else, and knows what you need in order to feel your pain and be able to integrate it into your story. I want to give you a look inside my sometimes internally chaotic world full of lies, anger, shame, hopeless despair, and grief so you can see me move toward truth, peace, joy, hope, comfort, and freedom.

I do not believe it to be chance that you are reading this book at this time. I believe you are being drawn into a new paradigm of living a more full and satisfying life. Your soul is naturally seeking to grow and mature. You know that you were created for relationship. You also know, however, that this is NOT an easy journey, nor a pretty one, nor a packaged one. The journey through our feelings toward God, toward our true selves, and toward others is crazy, unpredictable, and uncontrollable, but it is an adventure that rewards us with purpose and life-giving relationships that fill us with satisfaction and joy!

So, if you are ready, turn the page and let's step into the adventure together.

PART I

· · · · ·

*Sporadic Moments with the Divine
(1982-2005)*

In the Silence

July 2007

Made in Your image
A glory to bear
Yet distorted and dull
To the voice I must hear

Seeking, pursuing,
Diligently on
Your tender care so sweet,
Your persistence so strong.

A bright sun
A gentle breeze
Lovers dancing romantically
Beneath the trees

A heroic captain
Training his men
A terrifying warrior
Yet peaceful within.

To know Your mind,
To carry Your thoughts
The deepest challenge
given to man.

Yet in the silent,
Stillness, I know
And understand
That I can.

CHAPTER 1

Beginnings

I was probably nine years old the first time I sensed God's presence. It was 1982, the year I met Sara Murphy and the year I remember experiencing great loss. Sara and I were soul friends; she felt me, and I could read her mind. She had a lively personality and vibrant eyes that would light up when she smiled, which was often. I remember giggling incessantly till all hours of the night. In fact, I remember laughing, singing, and dancing every minute we were together. For the first time in my life, I felt I could be fully "me." For the first time in my life, I felt "not alone."

All of that came crashing down the day she left. We played up to the very last moment, and as I watched the moving van pull away, an emptiness formed in the pit of my stomach. I reached my hand out for her, toward her face pressing against the back window of the car. That's when it hit me: she was gone. Why didn't we exchange phone numbers or addresses or anything? We were 9! It never occurred to us, and apparently our parents never realized how important we were to each other. As the van drove out of sight, the sadness settled in that I would never talk to her again, much less see her. In a world without internet, we were lost from each other with an expansive country between us.

The empty feeling in my stomach began to rise; soon it would reach my throat and choke me, taking my very breath. I meandered into the deserted courtyard of our town-home complex. Something in me wanted to be alone, wanted the outside to match the depth of aloneness I was feeling on the inside. And, finally, the emptiness reached my eyes and tears began to form. "I am truly alone. I have no one now who understands me, no one who enjoys me fully, and no one to fully enjoy." The thoughts sought to take me captive into depression and hopeless despair.

Then something very normal, yet very holy, happened: a breeze. It was gentle, soothing, and personal. It was as if it brushed my face, almost lifting my head toward the sky, and I breathed deeply. And in that breath and on that breeze, I sensed God's presence. "You are not alone, My child. I am here."

One moment, I was about to be consumed with grief and despair, and the very next, I was filled with joy that the God of creation was with me and wanted to comfort me. I had heard about how much He loved me and wanted to always be with me, but those had been just words and longings. Now, in my deepest need, He had come. To my nine-year-old brain, it was that simple.

The joy bubbled up from within, and I began dancing around the courtyard, twirling in joy-filled sadness. It was a strange mix, but beautiful. I could mourn. I did not have to fear my sadness. I would not get lost in it, because I was so loved and I was not alone.

Little did I know I was surrendering myself to a truth that would serve me all of my life: Life is great loss, and joy is not the absence of pain, but the almost tangible presence of God in the midst of it.

*   *   *

The next time I remember sensing God's presence also involved deep, personal loss of someone I loved.

It was happening again... It was 1988 and I had found someone who loved me and enjoyed me completely. His name was John and he was my first real boyfriend. When I was with him, I felt alive, seen, and beautiful, and I laughed a lot.

Then the news came from John: "I'm moving back to California." How could this be happening to me again? This time, the emptiness invaded my entire body, mind, and soul. My childlike faith had turned to teenage doubt, and my brain could not quiet long enough to hear the Divine. After all, wasn't it Him allowing this to happen to me, again? Anger and sadness consumed me.

My family tried to reach me. My friends, too. But the pain was suffocating, and I needed to breathe. "Ending it all would end the pain, and I would be free." It was the razor in hand over the bathtub that set the stage for my next encounter with the Divine. In this desperate attempt to breathe, I heard His whisper again: "Toni, my precious girl, I can work ALL things for your good. I know that makes no sense to you now, but I am asking you to trust me... to trust that this pain will end, and to trust that I have a beautiful future for you. This pain will end, and your story will be well worth it. Will you trust me?"

I put the razor down and collapsed on the floor in a sobbing heap, the pain of helplessness and surrender violently wrecking my body. I would trust. I would walk the road of grief and look for Him there beside me.

I came to my feet weak and fragile, but calm. There was now a pureness to my grief. The anger was gone, the hopeless despair gone. Only sadness remained, accompanied now by hope. Hope that I would make it through this, because He said I would. Hope that, eventually, the emptiness in the pit of my stomach would be filled with His presence.

* * *

Twenty-four years later, my body still feels the wretchedness of loss, and it still demands resolution. Every time someone is taken from me, every time I have to move country, every time I am physically assaulted or robbed, every time my present is not what I thought it would be or what I want it to be, the pit of emptiness forms in my stomach and seeks to consume my very soul. Grief is like a black hole that pulls from within, sucking life into nothingness. I can get lost there. I *have* gotten lost there. And yet every time I cry out in my lostness, at some point there is a breeze, a still small voice that speaks my name, that calls me "precious", that says, "I know this hurts. I am here. Will you trust Me?"

Trust.

Ann Voskamp states so beautifully in her book *1000 Gifts* that "Trust is the bridge from yesterday to tomorrow, built with planks of thanks... Remembering is an act of thanksgiving, a way of thanksgiving, this turn of the heart over time's shoulder to see all the long way His arms have carried."

His arms have indeed carried, and the way has indeed been long. And it is not yet over. This ability to grieve is just the beginning, for I sense that when He says, "Trust me," He is leading me somewhere. I thought Jesus was on mission seeking and saving "the lost," but I have come to know that He is on mission seeking to save *all* that was lost, including parts of me that have been lost to even myself.

Experiencing Jesus as viscerally with me has been the beginning of a journey. But as you will see in the chapters that follow, this journey has at times taken me to even before these "beginnings" in order to heal the present and launch me into my future. And while the future is hopeful, I want my bridge of remembering to be strong enough to endure the losses I know are yet to come.

CHAPTER 1

For Personal Reflection and Practice

1. What is one memory you have where you were full of awe
    and appreciation? It could be a moment out in nature,
    coffee with a friend, the birth of a child, your wedding
    day, or a moment you sensed the presence of the Divine
    with you, etc....

2. Picture that moment in your imagination and reflect on
    how you felt physically. What did the temperature around
    you feel like? Were you sitting or standing? Who was with
    you? How did you react physically? Where you smiling?
    Laughing? Crying? Did you have lots of energy or were
    you calm?

3. Now, think about how you felt emotionally in that
    memory. Happy? Thankful? Excited? Humbled? Awed?
    Indebted? Loved? Cared for? Provided for?

4. If you feel you have a relationship with God, I invite you
    to thank Him for this memory. Every day this week,
    return to this memory in your imagination and enjoy the
    feelings again and again. Notice how you feel after
    remembering this memory.

CHAPTER 2

Returning to the Past
to Free the Present

February 1997 – Inviting Jesus into My Past

I have just finished a course on Theophostic Prayer Ministry (www.theophostic.com). It is a type of "prayer counseling" that invites Jesus to guide you to your past in order to find the damaging beliefs that lie within and hear God's perspective on what happened. It is fascinating to me. I am realizing that sometimes in the present when I get flooded with emotion, it could be because of a painful memory in my past that was never resolved or healed. Maybe I was left alone in my pain, or I believed an incorrect interpretation of what happened. Whatever the case may be, this feels so true and helpful. I will be open to letting Jesus take me back to the past if it means being freer in the present.

October 1997 – Out of Control

I am in Uruguay, SA. Matt and I have been through an amazing journey to get here. And we are finally here! Six years of preparation have led to this moment. We live in a small little apartment with no heat or air, no washing machine, and a camping stove to cook on. Life is not that easy, but I am just so glad to finally be here that I deny how hard it is... missionaries have it much harder in Africa, so how can I possibly complain?

But something strange is happening to me. Little things that Matt does can set me off into emotional oblivion. This has to stop. Why am I so easily triggered? I feel like a control freak! This last instance was too much.

I asked him to leave the hot water heater on so I could have a hot shower – a simple request, I thought. Water was pouring over my body before I realized that it was freezing! As the cold hit my skin, I flooded. Anger, guilt, self-hate, and disappointment bubbled up inside of me. I turned the water off and fumed. Matt had forgotten...

I ran to my room in a towel, and here I am writing. I don't want to hurt him, but I want to scream at him at the same time. I want to belittle him. I am angry, but there is more here than just anger. I am furious and disappointed at the same time.

I hear a voice inside that has a different perspective: "Anyone can make a mistake, Toni, so why are you so furious? Maybe this has more to do with YOU than him?" That voice makes sense. Maybe this is one of those moments where I need to look back in order to be freer now. My husband did not betray me or even try to hurt me on purpose. Maybe I need to listen more.

WHAT IS WRONG WITH ME?

"Jesus, I need you." I feel a little silly in my room writing, still wet from the cold shower and covered with only my towel, but I am desperate. "Here I am again in emotional overwhelm. Help!"

I call Matt in to sit with me here in this scary place. He knows the sting of my disappointment all too well, but he also knows that this is different. I am acting different. This is deeper.

Thankfully, he knows the questions to ask: "Toni, can you ask Jesus to take you to a memory where these emotions were present?"

My emotions race through my brain seeking the memory that has the same flavor. Bingo! 1982. Hot Springs Amusement Park. Arkansas. Family vacation. Roller coaster. I begin to relive this memory, in my mind, where I did not get to ride a roller coaster because I let someone else make a decision for me. I am overtaken with grief, anger, and disappointment. It was no one's fault. It just happened.

"I didn't get to ride the roller coaster." I manage the words between heaves of crying. I am immediately transported to the memory and feel as if it is happening in real time.

"What happened?" Matt gently prods.

My dad wanted to wait until nightfall to ride the roller coaster. He thought the lights would be beautiful from up top. I wanted to ride it first, but I agreed that it would be more beautiful to see the lights of the park at night. So, I quickly bounced away to the next ride, saving the best for last. A few hours later, we left the park for lunch, and upon returning, I notice the rides closing. It wasn't even dusk yet. This couldn't be happening. Panic struck in my chest. Confusion and fear pumped my body with adrenaline.

"Daddy, the rides are closing!" I yelled in a panic. "The park is closing! We have to get to the roller coaster!"

I took off running as fast as I could, heart pounding, up at least 15 flights of stairs to face the conductor. The roller coaster shoved off as I arrived.

"I want to ride, please can you make it go just one more time? We thought the park would be open longer!" The words were barely audible between gasps for air.

"No, ma'am, I am sorry. That was the last ride," he said, unmoved by my apparent devastation.

Shock.

Resignation.

I burst into tears and began the long decent to the bottom. I am sobbing as the memory is being relived in my imagination. I am fully there, even in the present.

"Toni, can you ask Jesus what you believed in that moment?" My husband's voice enters gently into my crisis.

I ask, and the story continues to play out in my mind, parts of the story I had never known before.

"I made a vow," I say. "I will never let anyone else make decisions for me. If I am in control, I will not get hurt."

As the words leave my lips, the pain of myself at 9 is unleashed into my 25-year-old body. Some part of me is afraid, and its shaming words flood my mind: "You must stay in control. You are such an idiot for trusting your dad back then, and you are an idiot for trusting Matt, now, with the hot water."

Anger, guilt, self-hate, disappointment – all directed at ME for trusting others. For the first time since I was 9, I begin to question that path.

"You cannot fully trust ANYONE but yourself!" A desperate voice comes across my mind in the present, and I realize this time, this voice is not my own. It is a voice that wants to destroy me, that wants to keep me bound in isolation.

"Toni," Matt lovingly intervenes, "can you sense Jesus there with you? Can you ask Him what He thinks about all of this?"

Yes. That is what I want to do. I ask. I wait. And then light in the darkness.

"Yes, He is here. I sense Him in the memory with me, walking me to the car. He is so sad for me. He understands why I believe what I believe, why I made this vow."

My Jesus is attuning with me. He is meeting me where I am, validating my hurt, seeing me.

As I begin reporting to Matt, the experience goes on. Jesus reaches down, looks me in the eye with compassion, and asks, "Is that working for you? Does controlling everything really keep you safe?"

I slowly shake my head no. He continues, "No matter what

you do, you still get hurt, don't you?"

Pain wracks my body again. My mind searches its memory banks to see if this is true. Yes. Yes, it is. Memory after memory surfaces, and I see that even when I am controlling everything, I still mess up and get hurt, or I hurt others. Flashes come to mind of how this has hindered relationships in my life. I didn't even let my husband choose my wedding ring for fear that I would be disappointed. Grief pours out my eyes. In my imagination, I am still standing with Jesus right there in the middle of the parking lot.

"Then what am I supposed to do, God?" I cry out for an alternate reality, a reframing of how to see the world.

"You can never be fully in control, Toni, but I can. I AM in control. Trust Me." Jesus gently invites me to reverse my vow and to trust Him instead of myself. He offers me His hand.

Wasn't this the real sin of Adam and Eve? Trusting *their* perspective instead of God's? Trusting my own judgment of what is best is not working for me. I am ready to try something new.

I can feel how paramount this moment is. I ask my 9-year-old self if she can give her hand to Jesus and walk with Him. We weigh the decision together.

The invitation to walk with Him in surrender is so much more appealing than the exhausted road I have walked for almost 20 years now, trying to control everything so I do not get hurt. It is useless and painful, and leads to me being alone.

The 9-year-old reaches for Jesus' hand and, upon contact, immediately finds comfort. My 25-year-old body relaxes and pours out tears of relief, tears of safety, tears of healing.

It is almost instant relief. I can rest. I do not have to diligently control and oversee every detail of life. I am free to rest. I am free to trust. I open my eyes for the first time since all of this began, and I see my husband's compassionate face looking back at me.

With his arms around me, he leans in and whispers, "I'm really sorry I turned off the water heater!"

"Thank you," I say laughing. But I know this moment was a

gift, an invitation to lean into something that has been going on inside of me from long ago, something that wanted resolution. Some part of me wanted truth, and it would continue surfacing until it found it.

I feel lighter, I feel free. Free to trust and free to get hurt. I am going to get hurt. I know I cannot stop it. But I can walk with Jesus through it and trust that it will not undo me.

This was the first time I discovered that there really are painful memories trapped in my soul that are affecting my present emotions and responses, because of the interpretation I believed in the moment. This was my first taste of the freedom that Jesus' truth brings. He said, "You will know the truth and the truth will set you free." I never knew what He meant until now. Now, I do.

"Knowing" the truth is not an intellectual activity. It is a visceral, almost tangible experience of Jesus speaking His perspective to me in the midst of my pain. It is His presence appearing to me and changing my emotional reality. His "truth" means nothing unless it is received into the non-verbal part of my being that feels, that remembers, that makes the vows, that hides from shame, that records truth as experiences, not words.

I want to know His truth and I want to be free.

CHAPTER 2

For Personal Reflection and Practice

For some people, going to the past is almost impossible. Few memories come, good or bad. If this is you, do not worry about your lack of access to the past. The past will come naturally as you build joy and appreciation. You do not have to go looking for it, necessarily.

For others, the past is so present that focusing on just the present is challenging. If this is you, do not worry about your overactive memories intruding into the present. You will be able to calm them as you build joy and appreciation.

For both types of people, as well as those who find themselves in between these extremes, trust the process you are entering into and please do not hesitate to seek professional help if necessary. As you reflect on the following questions, ask the Holy Spirit, our coach, to guide you and be with you during this time.

1. What part of this chapter caught your attention the most?

2. Do you find it hard to think about your past? If so, why?

3. Do you feel like you can embrace the complexity that even though someone has a "great" family, there will always be things that happened that will require grieving? What aspects of your family of origin are you thankful for? What aspects do you need to grieve or have you had to grieve? Do you feel like you have a safe community of people to enjoy you even when you are sad?

4. When you close your eyes and picture your family of origin around you, what do their faces look like? Do you see smiles of enjoyment? Or distracted looks? Anxious faces? Angry faces? How do their faces make you feel?

5. Have you ever over-reacted to a situation at hand, feeling more emotion then the current situation merited? Or, have you ever experienced someone else over-react to something that seemed insignificant to you? In either case, do you think the past could be affecting the way you or the other person is experiencing the present?

6. Return to your appreciation memory from your previous reflection time. Enjoy the memory again. If you feel up to it, look around in that memory and ask God where He was while you were enjoying that moment. Pay attention to any images, sensations, feelings, words, thoughts, or impressions that come to you and write them down. Don't analyze at this point just play with what comes to you.

7. After you have practiced listening, read over what you sensed. Is it consistent with who the Bible says God is? Does it bring peace and comfort? Share your appreciation memory with someone else, and tell him or her what you sensed from God, if anything.

If you did not sense anything, do not worry or get discouraged. This is why we call it practice. It is no small task to quiet your mind. For many of us this takes practice and time. Keep practicing remembering moments of thankfulness and appreciation. Thank God, try to sense what He thinks about that moment and how He felt during that time.

"Be still, and know that I am God." (Psalm 46:10)

"Be still before the LORD, and wait patiently for him." (Psalm 37:7)

"Be angry, and do not sin; ponder in your own hearts on your beds, and be silent." (Psalm 4:4)

"Be silent before GOD! For the day of the LORD is near." (Zephaniah 1:7)

The Gift of Difficult Relationships

November 1997 – Fear of Rejection

I have a problem with authority, with anyone "over" me. I cannot stand it when I do not have their approval. It is surfacing more and more as I interact with my boss and his wife here. I even lost a job over this issue when I was a bank teller a few years back.

I get nervous around them, scared of doing something wrong, scared they won't approve. What is going on in me? Where is this coming from? I *so* don't like living like this.

"Jesus, please let me know where this is coming from. Guide this process. I am so tired of feeling this way."

"What is it you are afraid of?" I hear the question formulate in my mind. Is this me or Jesus? I do not know, but it feels like healthy internal dialogue, so I will press in and indulge it.

"I am afraid of not doing it 'right,' whatever 'it' is! From washing dishes to cutting carrots, to leading worship or counseling someone. I cannot do anything right!"

"Okay," the wiser voice probes, "have you ever felt this before? Ask yourself if there are any memories where you felt scared of doing things wrong."

My mind begins to sift through the files of my soul looking for an emotional match. This is so interesting how my brain is doing this. I am anxious and fascinated at the same time. I focus on feeling "not-good-enough" and BINGO! My brain locks in on some memories that are actually quite painful.

My dad is here with me in my mind and I am hearing a myriad of comments coming from him like, "Can't you do ANYTHING right?" "You are such a butterfingers!" and "Well, that's the stupidest thing I have ever heard." As the words fill every inch of my mind, I begin to break down internally. I slump over and begin to cry.

"How does hearing all of that make you feel?"

"It makes me feel scared."

"Scared of what?"

I have to think about that one for a minute or two. Because you would think I would feel angry. But no, I'm scared. Scared of what? Scared of WHAT?

Finally, it hits me right between the eyes. "Of being rejected. I can't do anything right, and therefore I should be rejected!"

I am all ages, and these comments resound in my mind and define who I am, or who I think I am. Memories of trying so hard to be loved and accepted flow. No matter how much success, I still felt not good enough. I sob even more. It all feels so true. I cannot do anything right. I am reject-able. I am messed up.

"Where is Jesus?" A voice in my head speaks into my pain moving me forward.

I begin to look, to ask.

I sense Him here with me. Words form in my mind and images begin to unfold.

In my imagination, I am in the kitchen of my old house where I grew up. Jesus is there. He takes my hands. I am sobbing because I feel so incompetent. He looks me in the eyes and speaks into my pain in a way that only someone *inside* of me can. He is speaking directly to my wounded soul.

"You do not *have* to do everything right in order to be loved. I know that was the way you *felt* because of those comments and those moments with your father. But I am your Father, and I want you to know that you are loved just because you are MINE. You do not have to *do* anything to get My love, much less be perfect."

I feel held and soothed, and I stop crying. It is like a new path in my brain has just been carved, but it feels very new and extremely fragile.

I am loved, even if I am incompetent. My brokenness doesn't matter. I am still valuable. These words have been told to me all of my life since becoming a Christian at age 8, but this is the first time I have ever *felt* the difference they make inside of me. It is like Jesus has gone back in time and has begun to undo the wrong that was done.

He holds me now and wants me to rest. He knows I am exhausted after this journey. He also wants me to know that even when I am just resting, He still loves me!

October 1998 – Excluded

We have just arrived back in the USA from our one-year stint in Uruguay. We are staying with my husband's parents. They are so precious and kind, but our family culture is so different, and I am absolutely blown out of the water by what just happened to me.

I was studying and writing in my bedroom, waiting to be called for dinner, when I noticed that hours have passed, and no one has called. I go out of the room, curious that dinner was taking so long, only to find that they had already eaten without me. They did not even think to inform me or to invite me to join them.

I was furious! My family would NEVER have done this! My emotions are so strong that I have come back to the room to sort them, so as not to do or say anything I might regret.

41

What am I feeling? It is intense and deep. The pit forms in my stomach, I double over in pain, and the tears begin. I am frustrated with myself for feeling this strongly. I know family cultures are different. I know they did not mean to hurt me. But none of my logical thinking is working to make the pain go away. I have enough mental presence to ask myself what I need to know to get through this.

"What are you feeling?"

"Angry, unimportant, invalidated, like I am so unwanted that they don't even care if I am with them or not. They are fine without me. I am not wanted."

"Where is this coming from? Are there other memories where this emotion was present?"

My mind searches the memory files, and yes, it matches the emotions with a memory. I am 9 years old, maybe, and I am standing outside my big sister's door wanting to play with her and her friends. The door is closed, and I am not invited in. I hear words in my head, "Go away, we don't want you in here! Leave us alone!"

Did this happen? I really don't even know if my memory is telling me the truth. But what I do know is that my body, mind, and soul thinks it happened, so I continue with it, seeking resolution.

Rejected. Unwanted. Yes, those are the feelings. And here I am again in a situation where others are having fun without me and did not invite me to be a part of their evening. I feel unwanted and rejected.

The thought comes, "Are you really this pathetically needy? You are so weak."

I recognize this voice. It is not my own. It is a voice that seeks me harm. I ignore it and continue pressing into Jesus; I need to hear His perspective.

"Jesus, where were You that day at my sister's door?" I say out loud in hopes that He will come. Slowly, I look around in the memory and see Him there right beside me. He reaches out and pulls me to Him. I put my arms around His waist, burrow my head into His stomach, and wretch with grief as He holds me. No words are exchanged, but as I stay in His arms, weeping, an experiential truth is taking over my soul: someone wants me, and not just any someone, but the Creator of the universe is taking time to hold me and be with me. He must think I am important.

I have what I need to rest. I also feel like I can talk with the family now about what happened without flooding with anger from the past. I am wanted. I can explain to them why this hurt me so much and how I would love to be included in the future. I know it was not their intention to hurt me, and that it was God's intention to heal me through this gift of misunderstanding.

February 1999 – Voices from the Past

Five years of cleaning up after my husband, Matt, and I am at my end! When I see his clothes on the bathroom floor, his dirty dishes lying all over the house, and his shoes in the middle of the walkway, I am flooded with contempt. I could lash out at him, call him immature, and demand that he change. But, somehow, I am sensing that would not go over so well for our relationship. Also, I realize that this could be a gift for me.

I come today, my Creator, to ask for You to help me sort through all of this. I know that if I were not so emotionally affected by it, I could just have a conversation with Matt, ask him to take better care of his stuff, or set healthy limits for myself. However, I cannot even have this conversation because the emotions inside are way too strong. I am angry and I feel presumed upon. Can You show me what is going on?

Voices come to mind: "He is so inconsiderate! He does this just to bother you! He is presuming upon you and leaving all this work for you to do! He is such a slob!"

My anger builds as I hear all of this, but at the same time, I know these voices are not my own. I know Matt is none of these things. He cooks for me and bends over backward to listen to me, care for me, and love me. I feel ashamed, scared, and sad. I do not want to hurt my husband. I do not want to see him this way. I do not want to be so judgmental and condemning. These are my issues to be dealt with, but how do I get these thoughts out of my head? How do I change? Where is this coming from?

"Jesus, help," I cry to break the confusion.

So many memories flood my mind, memories of my father saying these very things to me and to my sister. I leave my book bag on the table and I am "inconsiderate" of others. I forget to put something away in the kitchen and I am "doing it just to bother" my dad. My dad was the same as me. Or, I guess I should say I am the same as him. That is why my dad isolates himself so much: He does not want to hurt us anymore, but does not know how to change.

I surprise myself because, instead of being angry at my dad for being this way, somehow I have deep compassion for him. I now know that he does not *want* to be this way, just like *I* do not want to be this way. It has been passed down to him to see people like this, to take things personally, just as he has passed it on to me. He hates this part of himself, just like I hate this part of myself.

Compassion overflows, and I begin to cry. My tears are like liquid prayer as I beg God for freedom for my dad, and for me. I know I need help. While there is room for Matt to grow, this is *my* growing edge. My shame is replaced with compassion for myself and my father, and I sense Jesus' approval of my conclusions. He wants me to get help, too. There are some skills that I am lacking in my relationships. I will go see a counselor for help.

March 1999 – Skill Learning

Matt and I went to see our Pastor for help. It was wonderful! He shared with us active listening or speaker-listener from the book *Fighting for Your Marriage*. For the first time in our nine years together we were able to fully listen to each other and hear what the other was saying. Matt finally felt safe enough to share what he is feeling on the inside, without fear that I would invalidate him. I finally felt like he heard what I was saying about my own process instead of hearing messages that I am not sending.

It seems that when I am struggling emotionally Matt blames himself for me struggling. Now, at least he can hear that *I* am not blaming him for my struggles. We will practice the skills laid out in this book faithfully: speaker/listener; time-outs; identifying negative communication patterns; talk-time; fun-time; etc. Thank you God for helpful help at this time!

October 2002 – Crazy-Making

We've been in Uruguay for the last two years and are now in the States on home assignment. Back in Uruguay I am facing a team explosion, economic shortfall, total vocational ambiguity, and, on top of all of that, I am having relational issues with a co-worker! She is psychologist to boot!

In spite of my desire to draw close to her, our relationship has been conflicted and difficult. She is a beautiful woman, incredibly intelligent, athletic, caring, nurturing, and passionate. And yet, every time I leave her after spending time together, I feel rejected, unloved, unappreciated, judged, and invalidated.

My heart is grieved. Her attacks come hidden, so subtle that there is hardly a way to confront her. And I am sensing that some of this problem is with me. I have somehow put myself under her and have been trying to prove myself to her. When I do not get her approval, I feel rejected, unlovable, and unworthy.

This reveals my fear. I am so afraid that people will get to know me and then reject me because of my rough edges. Why do I care? Why can't I be secure in who I am?

Then, in moments of pride, I try to stick up for myself and confront, but I end up hurting others. So I live in fear of either being judged and rejected by others, or hurting them without knowing it, and losing them because I have hurt them.

This is a crazy-making way to live. I feel trapped and alone. I am tired of fear and tired of being ashamed of who I am. I want freedom. I want to be able to love deeply.

After six months of trying to process this on my own, I am in my counselor's office.

"So tell me exactly what you are thinking and feeling," he probes again.

"I basically feel unlovable because I feel fake, selfish, and prideful. And I am afraid that others will reject me as soon as they get to know me," I blurt out succinctly for him.

"Hold onto those emotions and tell me if you have other memories where you have felt the same way." I know the routine by now and my mind begins the scanning.

I am 11 years old, and I meet my not yet brother-in-law for the first time. I was so excited that my sister was dating someone. I was finally going to get an older brother! I ran up to him in my 11-year-old excitement not realizing he was with his 15-year-old friends. In my memory, he made fun of me. It was a look or a comment, I can't remember what was said or done, but I remember walking away feeling stupid and reject-able.

"Are there any other memories?" the therapist continues to push.

I think I was 12 or 13. It was a snowy day. I was at home with my sister and this same boyfriend, now 18. "I do not know if what I remember is true or not," I let the counselor know. I really can't imagine this happening, but my mind has for some reason recalled its version of this memory.

"Just go with it," he reassures. "Something happened that was important. Maybe it was not exactly as you remember it, but the emotional content is what we are looking for anyway, not the specific details."

I continue in the memory. What unfolds is a fight between my sister and me. I would not move from in front of the TV so that she and her boyfriend could see, and in my version, she pulls me out of the way and kicks me. I end up on the floor in the fetal position crying in shock that she would do this to me. I get up and run to the neighbor's house and call my mom. I do not want to go home.

"What do you feel?" His questions annoy me.

"I hear the voice that something is wrong with me that my own sister did not love me. I am ashamed of who I am."

In another part of my soul, I know this is ludicrous! My sister loved and loves me very much. But for some reason, there is a part of me that cannot feel the love she has for me. This part of me is disconnected from the rest of me, it seems. I trust the process, hoping that in the end, all of me will know the truth.

"Where are you now?" The counselor realizes he has lost me into my own thoughts.

"I am selfish and prideful, and that is why others reject me. I am angry at God because, for 10 years now, I have been begging Him to change me and help me be more acceptable, and yet He does nothing!"

My cry turns to the Creator Himself, "WHY DO YOU SEEM SO POWERLESS?"

"You seem angry." The counselor states the obvious.

"Yes! I am angry, angry that all of this has happened in the first place. Angry that my sister and brother-in-law do not accept me, or that I do not feel enjoyed by them. Angry that my psychologist co-worker is so insidiously hurtful and gets away with it! That she thinks SHE is the healthy one, when she brags, avoids conflict, and makes other people feel like shit!" It feels good to finally get some of this off my chest.

"What do you want to DO with your anger?" the therapist calmly asks.

"I don't know. What do you mean?" I am clueless.

"Well, your anger is keeping you from sensing God's perspective right now. Do you want to hold onto the anger or release it?"

That is a duh kind of question, I think to myself, and I proceed to try to "release" my anger. But something inside me is holding onto it.

"I can't let go of it," I let the counselor know that I am stuck.

"What is your anger doing for you?" he prods.

That is a good question. What *is* my anger doing for me? I have no idea! I decide to ask Creator for help with this one. I know He knows my heart better than I do.

The answers begin to flow, "You are using it to protect yourself. You think that as long as you are angry, you can keep people from hurting you; that your anger will keep you at a distance and protect you."

I see myself with a shield around me, almost like a super power. I see how no one can get in and hurt me as long as I have this shield. It is tempting to hold on to.

"You are wrong," I hear the words whispered in my mind. God gently moves in to persuade me of the truth. "It will isolate you. As long as it is there, love cannot get in, and you will keep feeling unlovable, reject-able, prideful, and insecure. Is that what you want, Toni?"

I hate it when He reads my mail. I can see that as long as this shield is in place, I look safe. Yet the only thing it really blocks is the love that is trying to get to me.

Then, I see Him there in my imagination, my Creator, my Maker, the One who knows how I was intended to function. He is there just outside of my shield. I feel invited into a different way, a way I had not seen before. Do I want to keep my shield of anger?

"No. I do not want that for my life." I respond in tears, knowing that the step before me will be a point of no return into the unknown.

"Give it to Me and let ME protect you. I will not keep you from being hurt, but I will heal your wounds. I will give you freedom and life." Jesus softly and gently pleads with His hand outstretched in front of me.

I let go. And in some strange way, it feels like a hostage

situation has just been defused, and my soul has been freed.

"Now what do you feel?" asks the therapist eagerly.

"I feel sorry for her, for my co-worker. She is living in her pain, and she doesn't even know it. She will destroy herself and her relationships this way. I can see so clearly now how she is wrong, how it has nothing to do with me. I pity her."

"Would you be willing to ask Jesus what He thinks about that?" replied the therapist.

All of a sudden, I am Eve again in the Garden of Eden. Do I trust my own judgment or do I seek Creator's perspective? We were never meant to judge for ourselves without His perspective. Ours is so limited, so narrow. His is eternal and all-knowing. I have been here before. We have been fools throughout history to not ask His perspective. I ask.

I sense Creator come to my co-worker's defense. "I am working in her, too. You don't have to feel sorry for her or pity her. That's your way of elevating yourself over her to try to puff yourself up again. Let my love for you be enough."

His confrontation is not offensive. He is not harsh. He is loving and understanding. And He is right. I can see that He loves her, too, just as much as He loves me. She, too, was created in His image.

"But if I do not pity her, what is my response to be?" I ask, not knowing the way forward.

"Compassion," He answers. "She is doing the best she can with what she has to work with. She will learn more skills with time, just as you will. Trust Me and have compassion on the weakness you see."

That feels good. It feels right.

"What about the memory with your sister?" The counselor suggests I return there and see what Jesus might want me to know.

Some of the pain of rejection returns. How can my own sister not love me?

Jesus knows my pain. He is there in the room with us where the fight took place. He kneels to the floor where I am in the fetal position, my sister over me. He grabs my sister's hand and places it in mine. We look at each other.

"I am so sorry this happened to you both," He laments. "You both were just living out the dysfunction of the world you were in. I am so sorry you both were hurt. In time, I will heal you individually, and I will heal your relationship with each other, as well."

As I feel my sister's hand in mine, the feelings of rejection dissolve. The tension in my shoulders fades away, my lungs expand, my pulse slows, and my body is at peace.

My understanding of what happened has changed. I now feel the reality that we both lacked the skills to navigate all that was going on in us and between us. I cannot yet feel that she loves me, but I can at least feel compassion for both of us and know that it was not about me being unloved or reject-able. It was about something so much bigger than us.

CHAPTER 3

For Personal Reflection and Practice

As you can see in this chapter, most of the time, people I find difficult are not just causing problems for me in the present, but they are unintentionally stirring up issues that already exist from my past. As I choose to look within and see what pain they could be triggering, they become a gift.

1. Breathe deeply, close your eyes, and give yourself some time to find an appreciation memory. What is a memory where you felt thankful, or safe, or full of awe? It can be the same one you have been working on in previous chapters, or a new one. As before, think about what you felt at that moment emotionally, but also physically.

2. Ask Jesus where He was during that moment in your life. Pay attention to sensations, feelings, thoughts, and impressions. Look around the memory and see if you can actually see Him. What does His face show you? How does He feel about being with you?

3. Now, staying in your appreciation space, ask yourself and Jesus if there is any relationship that seems particularly difficult for you right now. What feelings are being triggered by that relationship? Share all of your feelings with Jesus. Hold none back. He can handle whatever it is you need to say.

4. Ask Jesus if there is anything He would like you to know about this situation. Write down whatever you hear, and continue back and forth with Him (or yourself if you do not clearly sense Jesus, yet) until you have better clarity on what is going on and what you need to do to respond well.

5. Return to your appreciation memory and rest in those feelings you find there.

CHAPTER 4

The Power of Silence

August 2003 – Biblical Imaginative Play

Back in June, I started practicing silence, as Dallas Willard indicates in his book *The Spirit of the Disciplines*. I know I need this practice. I sense a turbulent world on the inside of me causing all kinds of chaos, draining my energy. I want to learn to quiet.

Also, my imagination is coming to life for the first time since I was a child! I wonder if this is part of what Jesus meant when He said the Kingdom of God is for children, and we must become like a child to enter in?

Today, I am meditating on Psalms 45-47. As I read, I am drawn to ask Jesus to show me what He looks like. The Psalmist writes almost as if he can see the very face of his King. Papa, I want to play like that with you, to enter into the unknown and let you use my imagination to show me the unseeable. Show me Yourself, please.

As I give my imagination to the Divine, I begin to see Him! This is what I see:

Oh my King, handsome and beautiful.
Your face is one of honor.
Pain, You have known, yet in the midst of it, You were true.
Your face is one of grace –
You look on us with love and delight.
Your face is one of mercy –
You hurt for us and long for us to overcome.
Your face is one of joy –
You take joy in me. You are glad to see me.
Your face is one of power –
You protect us diligently. You will avenge us one day.
You wear glory as Your crown.
Our faithfulness brings You glory for it is You who keeps us faithful.
If I could kiss Your feet a thousand times my heart would overflow with joy.
Never needing to look at Your face my heart would be content just holding Your feet.
And yet, You lift me up with Your gentle, firm hand.
You tilt my face upward toward Yours.
As I see Your face I am completely exposed.
I try to hide, to escape Your gaze.
I want to run, but I cannot flee.
I cannot move. I am frozen, completely exposed.
All that I try to hide from others, You see.
But, You are not ashamed of what You see in me.
And as I look into Your eyes, the shame I feel for who I am disappears.
Your face...
You think I am beautiful. I am worth Your love. I am Yours. I collapse again at Your feet, grasping them with both arms. I am afraid You will leave me.

"Don't go!" I cry out. "Dwell with me!"

You pick me up with one arm and, swinging me around, place me on the back of Your black horse. I cling to You with all of my heart and strength, my King. I do not care where we go, or what happens to me in the process for You are with me. You love me. Let me feel the warmth of Your body. Let me see Your face, and I will be at peace always.

But wait! Where are You taking me?

There is a cave, a group of people are there, protected in the cave.

No, my King, don't leave me with THEM!

He has stopped so that I can dismount and join these other people.

"What? What are you doing?" I ask desperately.

"I am leaving you here for now. These people are to be My hands and feet to you. I need to go get others who are lost, My child," Jesus says. "You are to love one another."

"We do not know how to love!" I scream at Him. "We are broken! We will hurt each other!"

I have known the difficulty of relationships. I know all too well that we humans know nothing of love. Even those of us who name the name of Christ are just as unhealthy in the ways we relate. I have seen too much hidden in church communities. I have seen the subtle abuse of control, guilt, and manipulation. I am done. I want nothing of them. I also know myself. I know I am incapable of truly loving them, as well. I will hurt them, too.

"How can what You are saying be true?" I plead with Him to reconsider, to help me understand.

"They will be My physical body to you.

In them you will see My face.

They are beautiful, and I love them deeply.

I want you to love them, too.

I know you have been hurt by other Christians, but you must open your heart to My people again, it is the only way."

"I will hurt them, my King. I would rather die a thousand

deaths than be exposed before them. They will gossip, they will judge, they will give unwanted advice, they will never understand me, nor seek to understand me."

The truth comes out: I am afraid, and I have been hiding.

"There is no other way, Toni. Do not fear, for I have redeemed you. I have called you by name. You are Mine." His words from Isaiah 43 resound loud and clear in my mind. He has redeemed *us*. He has called *us* by name. We are His. I cannot exist alone in my faith world. Somehow I belong to a larger "we" that is beautiful, that is redeemed, that is called by God. I do not like this way at all. It is risky. It is imperfect. It means pain.

"I am with you," my Jesus reminds me, just as He had reminded His disciples before He had left them. "Love them. Reveal yourself, and do not fear."

He slides me off the horse and turns to leave. I know He is going after someone else who is lost in the desert of isolation. He is finding His lost sheep.

I stand there in shock and slowly turn to see those He has left me with. I turn to begin to trust again.

Strange how His mission is to restore what was lost inside of me, but also between my community and me. And somehow they are related: my inner healing and my ability to live maturely in relationship with others.

November 2003 – Many Mindsets

Four months of practicing quieting my mind, and today, I see all of the emotional states of myself in a white room, represented as various "people" chatting incessantly. One is angry, one is quiet and feels lonely, one is loud and arrogant. I do not understand them all, but I am trying to just get them to be quiet! Every day for ten minutes, I sit and invite these different emotion states to quiet and to try to listen to Jesus. Where is His voice? I cannot begin to hear Him when so much is going on inside of me.

December 2003 – Quiet

Today, after five months of practicing silence, I succeeded in quieting all these "voices" inside. I shoved them into the closet in the white room! Somehow I sense this is not the best way to deal with all of them, but they were finally quiet!

January 2004 – Joy

I began reading *The Life Model: Living from the Heart Jesus Gave You* by Dr. James Friesen, Dr. Jim Wilder, Anne Bierling, Rick Koepcke, and Maribeth Poole. It is revolutionary in its teaching. I have finally found others who are having an intelligent discussion based on good psychology *and* biblical faith.

Based on what I have read, I realize that joy is going to be crucial to every part of my healing, including trying to quiet myself. Wilder says joy is "the feeling you get when someone is glad to be with you no matter what." It also seems to be the glue that can integrate the different facets of my soul.

I need to hear them, all of these "voices" inside of me. They need to be heard. They need to know that someone is glad to be with them no matter what! They are angry, sad, scared, ashamed, disgusted, and hopeless. They need to be heard, valued, and accepted, *not* ignored and shoved into a closet!

As I realize this, I ask Jesus to come into the room. I have been trying to get myself together so I could hear Him. It never occurred to me that He could help me quiet! I need to introduce each facet of myself to Him, and let Him teach me how to listen to and love myself. This feels like an important step in my growth and development.

February 2004 – The Merge

Every day, I have been spending time listening to myself and letting Jesus soothe and quiet all of the different emotional facets within me. What an amazing experience of "Be still and know that I am God" (Psalm 46:10). Receiving from Jesus in this way is so different than striving to *do* something for Him. I am seeing the importance of taking the time to let *Him* do for me! This feels right and good. It feels transformative!

Today, I sensed the different emotional states in my white room stand up and merge into one person! I am now one in the white room and quiet. I do not know what that means, but it feels strong, beautiful, whole, integrating. Like the fragments of my soul that have been blown apart because of the Fall are now being put back together again, joined by joy: Jesus being glad to be with me and *me* being glad to be with me no matter what.

June 2004 – A New Creation

Eleven months of practicing quieting myself almost daily. In my time of silence today, I saw an amazing thing happen. In my imagination, I was in my white room where I sense the innermost parts of my soul, all of us in one. Today, Jesus was there with me, and, without words, He enveloped me, His body over mine as if to hold me. Then, we merged into one, stood up tall, and walked right out of that room together, a new creation. I do not know the implications of this in my life, but I feel free, strong, *not* alone. I feel Him with me in a new way, close by. Verses are coming to my mind, and for the first time in my life, I feel what these verses are getting at. This is real. He is real.

> "Therefore, if anyone is in Christ, he is a new creation. The old has passed away; behold, the new has come." (2 Corinthians 5:17)

"Or do you not know that your body is a temple of the Holy Spirit within you, whom you have from God? You are not your own." (1 Corinthians 6:19)

"And it is God who establishes us with you in Christ, and has anointed us, and who has also put his seal on us and given us his Spirit in our hearts as a guarantee." (2 Corinthians 1:21-22)

"And we all, with unveiled face, beholding the glory of the Lord, are being transformed into the same image from one degree of glory to another. For this comes from the Lord who is the Spirit." (2 Corinthians 3:18)

"But we have this treasure in jars of clay, to show that the surpassing power belongs to God and not to us." (2 Corinthians 4:7)

My response is worship and thankfulness. How do *we* work, Papa? Show me, my King.

September 2004 – He is Already Pleased

I am away. I have come to be alone with Creator in silence and solitude for three days. I am nervous and excited. Time stops, and there is nothing to fill the void: no radio, no TV, no friends, and not even my own voice. Only my thoughts and His are here to entertain me.

I am reading through the Psalms and realizing a pattern I want to enter into. It seems like whenever the Psalmist is in distress, he starts off being honest with God about his emotions. There is *no* shame. He knows God is glad to be with him no matter what.

Then he remembers the works that God has done in his past. He recounts them to himself, tells them to others. And finally this remembering leads him to trust in God's character even if he does not understand what God is doing or why.

Be honest about your emotions, remember, and trust.

Be honest. I am realizing that I am plagued by a part of me that guilts me over everything. If I don't get up early to be with You, if I take naps, if I enjoy myself, if I lay out and enjoy the sun, there is a part of me that feels guilty, like I am afraid of displeasing You.

I feel guilty for having too many clothes, too much sleep, too much food. There is so much need around me. But what is too much? Will I ever feel like I can meet my own needs? Or, do I have to give everything away and live in suffering in order to feel like I am pleasing You? I have already left my church, my family, my country to serve You; what more do I have to give up to feel "enough"?

Where is freedom in this? Where are *You* in this? What do I need to know?

Remember. I see the image of You with me in my white room. You hear me. You care. You are tender and loving. You envelope me and make me stand strong.

"Toni," I hear my Maker whisper in my ear, "This part of you is trying to guilt you into doing better/being better because it thinks you will feel more loved if you are living perfectly. It wants to help you, but it is actually hurting you."

"Oh, Papa, I do not want guilt to motivate me. I appreciate all that this part of me does to try to help me feel close to You, but what does it need to know?"

"This part of you needs to know and experience that I am already pleased with you! You do not have to earn My pleasure, but you do have to receive it. You need to let Me enjoy you. I want My enjoyment of you to be what motivates you to press on. Remember, that was My motivation: 'for the joy set before' Me, I endured the cross. *My enjoyment of you will be the only thing powerful enough to sustain you through what is to come.*"

I feel Jesus smile over me, and it feels freeing, yet

uncomfortable. It feels expansive, yet exposing. I stay here and try to let it in, but I know this will take time.

I am brought back to the physical world. I am sitting on a hill overlooking the ocean. The palm trees are beautiful bursts of green dotting the landscape below, and the breeze is refreshingly cool. I look down to the beach below, and I see stones, like little islands, longing for the water to come and cover them, to saturate them with life before the heat of the day ignites them all.

"That is you, My child." I sense His words over me. "You are a stone, one little stone out of so many. But one that wants to be bathed in My life-giving water, so that when the heat comes, you will have Me to release to the world. You will have My steam, My presence in you manifesting through you to those around you. The stones without water only get hot and burn others. There is no steam. I want to bathe you in My enjoyment of you, letting it run over you like water over these stones. And you will give hope to the world when the heat comes."

His words are encouraging. I know He is changing me, but change seems so slow going. I will let myself soak and try to be patient.

CHAPTER 4

For Personal Reflection and Practice

In this Section of the book it becomes apparent that as soon as I draw closer to God, He moves me into community. And, as soon as I move into community, I am faced with the weaknesses that God wants me to work on or wants to heal. Then, as he heals me, He enables me to move deeper into Him and into His people. It is indeed a painful, and yet beautiful, joy-filled dance between the three: Community, Maturity (things I need to work on), and God's Healing touch. Silence surrounds all of these relationships and gives me the space I need to reflect and listen.

1. How would you best describe how you feel about sitting in silence?
   - What's *that*?
   - Afraid of it.
   - Hesitant.
   - Curious.
   - Longing for it.
   - Enjoying it regularly.

2. Take three minutes right now and practice quieting your mind. If you are like I was when I began, you may want a little guidance on how to do this. Dr. Dan Siegel was a tremendously helpful resource for me. For Dr. Siegel's "breath-awareness" practice, as he calls it, go to (www.drdansiegel.com/resources/everyday_mindsght _tools). There are other resources on his page as well for deepening your practice of silence.

3. Of the three dynamics mentioned above (Community, Maturity, and God's Healing touch), ask yourself and God which you are being invited to move towards at this time

in your life. How does He want you to do so? What resources do you need?

4. Share with two people what you are sensing God saying.

It Takes Time Sometimes

August 2005 – Waiting

The 1997 song "Takes a Little Time" by Amy Grant and Wayne Kirkpatrick keeps going through my mind. It is a song that compares a relationship to the Titanic, in the sense that when a relationship hits a difficult bump, it takes time to turn it around and get out of dangerous waters. I particularly like the hopefulness in the song when they say that even though it takes more than they have to offer right now, they still know their relationship is not "going down".

At the end of 2003, three years after arriving back in Uruguay, Matt suffered a nervous breakdown. I cannot begin to try and explain all of the factors that contributed to his emotional and nervous system collapsing, but suffice it to say that it was a very painful experience for all involved. We were in an emotionally hostile environment with very little help, professional or otherwise. And, we had a three-year-old daughter depending on us for her mental health and stability.

I think my soul went into some sort of lockdown, hence the

white room that represented me in my imagination. I felt safe there. Those daily times of quieting kept me sane and allowed grace in, because, honestly, I don't think I was receiving it from anyone else.

As Matt has slowly recovered, I have struggled to support him, keep the ministry going, care for our child, and try to meet my own needs. For the past two years, even though I have been learning to quiet myself, I have felt blocked emotionally, relationally, and vocationally. I feel numb.

Almost daily, I have begged God to remove what is hindering me. I have confessed anger and contempt toward Matt and toward coworkers. I have worked hard at loving others, even when they mistreated me. But, somehow, none of this has opened my soul to receive again.

So, I wait. Wait for my heart to find the safety it needs to come forth and share with me what is blocking it. Is this what the Spanish mystic, St John of the Cross, called the "dark night of the soul"?

September 1, 2005 – Exposed

We are in Memphis on furlough. It has been a whirlwind of hugs, laughter, conversation, and activity. We are with our dearest mentors, John and Jamy. I am so very thankful for them in my life. We survived Uruguay for a year together back in 1998. They know what we experience living there, how hard it is, how isolating. We also know them, the battles they have fought, even the ones they've lost.

They know us all too well, though, and I am feeling exposed. They have a way of seeing deep within my soul. What if they see what is hidden from even my own eyes? I feel like I am unintentionally hiding a part of me from everyone right now, mainly because I do not even know what is going on inside. I feel overly sensitive, shut down, critical of Matt, and afraid that John and Jamy will see that something is not right. They see it all. There really is no hiding. I hate it when others see my weaknesses that I am unaware of. Image control goes out the window, and I fear they will judge me and reject me. Help me, Father. I need you so badly. I am afraid.

September 2, 2005 – Turning Around

Today, we began to share with John and Jamy all that happened during Matt's 2003 breakdown. I was having flashbacks of events that had occurred as I began recounting.

"That is so strange," I shared. "I am feeling so connected with everything that happened, like my body is remembering."

"That happens," Jamy responds. "When we approach the anniversary of any trauma we have experienced, it is like we process it again at deeper levels."

Is that what was happening to me? My soul opened at the thought, and I felt safe. I could see our friends were not judging us, they were happy to be with us, even in our pain. They wanted to share in our sufferings with us. It was almost like Jesus was in the room touching me through them, using their eyes to show me His deep sorrow and love for me.

After two years of numbing, the anger, fear, and betrayal I had felt during Matt's meltdown finally found light in the safety of this circle. Knots formed in my stomach, and tears flooded my eyes as my brain put words to all of the difficult moments we had lived during those six months of confusion. I do not blame my husband for all of that. We were in it together, like a bad car accident that left everyone injured and unable to help each other.

Ideas started to form in my mind, new ideas that seemed to explain what was happening deep within. "Toni, what you went through was so painful you were not able to feel it without more joy in your life. You have been living in a joy-deficit, so to speak. Also, while you don't want to blame your husband, the truth is that you are believing lies about him, so that you do not have to move toward trusting him again. Part of you is scared this will happen again. That is part of what has been blocking you."

Is this Jesus? I am not sure, but I have come to believe that any truth that comes in and changes the way I perceive reality usually is my Creator leading, healing, guiding. I decide to engage. "What lies do I believe?" I ask in my mind as my friends pray over me.

Tears continue to flow as accusations toward my husband form into words for the first time ever and leave my lips: "Matt is a workaholic who cannot control himself and will never put me or our family first. I cannot open myself up to him. He makes decisions out of his pain, not out of listening to Jesus. I cannot trust him. I am on my own."

Silence consumes the room as these words echo in my mind. I am shocked. How could I think this about the man who has given his very life to love me? Relationships are so complicated, and I know all too well that I am not innocent. My controlling, contemptuous pride has marked him, I am sure of it.

I also know this is part of trauma, a distorted view of reality. I need to embrace these feelings to get through them. I let myself feel the full weight of them. I verbally acknowledge again what I have secretly believed as true. "I cannot open myself up to him. I cannot trust him, and therefore, I am on my own."

Hopeless despair sweeps over me. It feels heavy, almost crushing. I slump down in my chair and reach for my friends around the table. I need combined joy-strength to face this level of despair deep inside of me. Without words, they lovingly take my hands and begin to cry with me. It feels freeing to finally get the secrets out, to finally know what was within that I could not see.

In this very intimate and intense moment, I sense my Maker speak His truth, "My child, these accusations about Matt may feel true at times. Yes, your husband struggles, but this does not define him, nor is it all of him. He is not a victim of his pain."

I can now see Jesus in my imagination. He draws close and

pulls me into His arms.

Part of me resists. All of the hurt, anger, confusion, and loneliness from two years ago is surfacing and screaming that I am right, that Jesus is mistaken, that my husband will choose numbing his pain over relationship again, and that I will be left to put the pieces back together.

"This does not have to be the case, Toni," Jesus defends him. I open my eyes and look at my husband there around the table with my dear friends. His eyes are compassionate toward me. I glance at our friends. They know our pain. They have walked this road and worse. They know how hard it is for me to trust again. Matt has let himself be exposed before them, so that I could find healing. That takes courage and strength. My respect for him grows. He is here, listening, trying to understand.

"As long as you believe these things to be true about your husband, you will find evidence against him, and this will be your only experience of him. But, if you let go, you will be able to see the truth, and it will set you free."

"What is the truth, Father?" I ask, begging for a different reality.

"Your husband loves you so much. He has been working very hard to be fully present with you, Allie, and himself. These are new skills for him, and it is not easy. But, because of your protective stance, you only see the moments he fails. You are not seeing all the times he is longing for you and making time for you. Also, he is working hard to seek Me and not make decisions out of his pain. He is in relationship with others, as well, and he is seeking professional help. You have to be willing to listen and believe the best."

His words crack through the lies I have been holding on to. I want to see the truth, to see what is really happening in him, in us. I do not want to hold on to beliefs that will keep me isolated and alone. I do not want fear to control me.

"I forgive you, Matt." As the words leave my lips, I feel the distance between us removed. He knows now how deeply his actions affected me. I am not the strong one who can bear all. I have my breaking points, too.

"I am so sorry, my love, for all of the pain I put you through back then. I am committed to getting help for myself."

"I am sorry, too, Matt, for fearing you these past years, sorry for only seeing when you fail. I let go of this thinking, and I commit to seeing you the way God sees you."

As we embrace, these blessed friends come around us as if to bandage the wounds and protect the new growth that is happening within us and between us. They are so happy to be a part of what God is doing in us. They are proud of us for doing the hard work of stewarding our pain well.

They explain, "When you live through trauma the way you two have, it takes a little time sometimes to recover all that was lost. It takes being safe and being with people who are glad to be with you in your pain. It takes being willing to hear Jesus' perspective, as well. We are so glad we could be here. Please call us next time anything like this is happening."

I am not sure why we did not call on them two years ago during the breakdown. I guess we were so used to having to do life alone, that it never occurred to us to cry out for help. We are still getting used to the thought that there are some people out there who can handle our pain without needing to trivialize it, or fix us, or blame us. People who are glad to be with us and close enough to the Divine that they can hold space for us to hear His voice and sense His presence.

Thank You, Papa, God. Thank You for our friends, our mentors. Thank You for the safety my soul has received in order to reach the depths of pain and lies that have had their hold on me. Thank You for their stories that give us understanding and hope. Thank You that I am not alone, that we are not alone.

I feel our relationship is like the Titanic, so many underwater places that can get injured and take the ship down, and so slow to change direction and recover from a hit. Thank You for the perspective that some things take time to turn around, and thank

You for the hope that we are not going down!

CHAPTER 5

For Personal Reflection and Practice

No matter how diligent I am about growing, some processes take more resources than I have in the moment. Yet, when the time is right and there is enough safety, my soul opens if I let it. But it is only because of *practicing* listening, quieting, and sensing Jesus with me that I can risk opening up to those around me.

1. List the people who you feel safest with, those who enjoy you the most, who do not judge you, who do not need to "fix" you; those who are able to listen and ask good questions that help you discover things about yourself that you did not know.

2. Write them a note thanking them for being safe for you. I have found these people to be few and far between. If you have some in your life, thank God for them and thank them. Chances are they have done some very difficult maturing work to become safe people.

3. If you cannot think of any people like this in your life, pray for God to bring you some and pray that God will make you one! I know that many times during my journey I honestly could not think of people who were safe for me, but they were there. I just could not see them. God wants you to have healthy relationships, and He is our Provider!

PART II

• • • • •

*Discovering Wholeness
(2006-2010)*

A Bird at Play

September 2007

What fun it must be being you!
Soaring, gliding, glazing, diving –
You fly so low your wings almost touch the water.
Are you looking for food?
Or are you just enjoying yourself?

There's an amazing beauty to your flight
Elegant, smooth, silent, swift.
You are playful.

I see you dancing way up high
before you come back down
to glide over the water's face,
Almost caressing it, teasing it.

What fun it must be being you.

CHAPTER 6

Intent versus Impact

April 18, 2006 – Misunderstood Intentions

"So, I am wondering if Silvia can join our group." I had just made a plea to our women's missionary small group to open itself up to one more person. We were five in total and, in reality, only two of us were remotely emotionally stable. I was hoping that bringing Silvia into the group would add greatly needed maturity and stability.

"Absolutely not!" Margaret stated definitively without even thinking it through.

"I am against it as well," added Denise.

I look to Ann, our leader, for some sort of sanity, and I realize she has frozen in the face of this conflict.

I am on my own here, I think, and my heart rate quickens. "Would you at least be willing to pray about it, and ask Jesus what He wants for us?" I plead one more time.

"No," they replied.

Wow! I honestly cannot believe this is where we are. I am infuriated with these so-called "women of God" that I work with. I do not understand their stance. My anger keeps me from being able to engage them in a healthy conversation, so I journal.

The more I think about it, the more I sense that while my intention was to bring safety and stability to our group, they have received my actions as offensive and threatening to their security. I am now the enemy.

This tends to happen frequently in our work meetings. I have one intention that is to love, to help, to add value, or to protect, but instead of seeing my heart, the group lashes out at me as if I had attacked, betrayed, taken, or harmed. Somehow the impact I have on them is different than my intention. The others judge my motives without seeking understanding, and I am caught trying to defend myself to them and explain my heart.

I absolutely *hate* working in an environment like this. My mentors would call this a low-joy environment, so little trust. I flood, and I want to just leave them all. I manage to physically stay in the group, but I go subterranean in my soul, searching for the way forward. I get lost again in my internal emotional world.

What part of this cycle is mine? I know it is my maturity task as an adult to help others understand my own thoughts, feelings, and needs. But I get so triggered that I lose the ability to stay engaged with them, and then, I shut down. It is like my brain dis-integrates, or falls apart. I cannot sense any joy, and I lose myself in shame and anger. I cannot get to the cause of all of this. It is too complex for me. Please help, Papa.

April 19, 2006 – Protected

I am here with a friend who is a therapist, as well. She is here for a short time from the States. I am so thankful for those who come on occasion to help support us. She is willing to sit with me and guide this process of following Jesus into whatever is connected to the current situations I find myself in with my team.

"What is your strongest feeling?" June asks as we begin.

I quiet. I sift my emotions. "Fear. I am afraid… afraid of being exposed… afraid of unintentionally hurting someone… afraid of others talking about me behind my back, distancing themselves from me, or shaming me and ultimately rejecting me." Physically, I want to simultaneously hide and attack. My adrenalin rushes and I am ready for a battle.

"Jesus, can you please lead Toni to whatever memories might be connected?"

I knew that was the next step. Some memories surface from high school and college.

"I was on a youth retreat in Florida with our high school youth group, and I was hurt deeply by supposed friends."

"Can you share what happened?" June invites.

"Yes, I was dressing for the luau, and I didn't know if what I was wearing was appropriate or not. I often struggled in Christian circles with what clothing was 'appropriate.' In my public school environment, I was considered conservative, but in my Christian context, apparently I had a hard time being conservative enough!

"At any rate, I asked my adult counselor for her advice on what I was wearing. Was it okay? Was it too tight or too sexy looking? She said she thought I looked fine, and so I left for the luau confident that I was appropriately dressed.

"As I boarded the bus, however, two girls sitting on the front row thought otherwise and commented loud enough for me to hear, 'Wow, someone looks like a slut.'

"I was crushed. My intention had been to respect this environment and the people gathered there. But, obviously that was not how they interpreted it.

"I backed up and looked at those two girls. 'I am so sorry if I have offended you,' I said honestly. 'My intention was not to look slutty today. And your comment was hurtful and uncalled for.'

"I continued down the aisle and joined my friend in the seat next to her, but emotionally I was spinning. Somehow, I managed to collect myself enough to enjoy the luau. But, afterward, as soon as I arrived back in my condo, I told my room counselor what had happened on the bus and asked her about my outfit again. This time, she confessed that she thought it was a little too tight, and that she was sorry she didn't have the courage to tell me earlier."

Tears flow for this teenager who was trying her best to belong, to "get it right," but was shamed anyway.

"What did you do after that?" June inquires.

"Well, I went and talked with the girls. I told them the whole story, explained how their comment had hurt tremendously, and explained that if they consider themselves followers of Jesus, they might need to reevaluate how they treat people. Their behavior definitely did not draw me to Christ in them. They apologized profusely, and I won two friends that day. But it still hurts."

"What about the other memory?" June moves me forward.

"Token time," I say remembering the phrase one of my dearest friends had used to criticize me. "Our college group was on a Florida retreat. The boys had telephoned our cabin to invite a few of us girls over. Tim was talking to me on the phone and asked Terry, my friend, if they wanted me to come over, too. Tim did not realize that the mute button did not work, and I heard Terry say, 'No, we don't want her!'"

I pause as the feelings of betrayal and rejection sweep over me. We were like brother and sister. At least, he was like a brother to me. I guess I have no idea what I was to him.

June realizes I am getting lost in thought. "So, what happened next?"

"Well, later that night I asked Terry if we could talk. I told him that I had heard the conversation, that I was confused and deeply hurt.

"'You give people token time, Toni.' He excused his actions by criticizing me. 'A little glance here, a comment there. That is all we get from you. Token time.'

"I stood there so confused, hurt, and feeling betrayed. Apparently, they had been talking about me behind my back for some time now, and I honestly did not even understand his criticism. No one had ever sought to understand my side of things,

Also, if I was doing something wrong or hurtful, at least they could come to me and talk with me about it, not gossip behind my back. I was worth more than that, we all are."

As the pain sweeps over me, June turns to prayer, "Jesus, is there another memory even older that is similar to these?"

"Yes." The memory comes, and I physically pull my legs up into a ball in the chair and begin heaving in pain.

"I am 9, I think. My father and I had just had a fight downstairs, and feeling shamed and attacked, I ran upstairs, threw myself on the bed, and began to sob. I had felt so mistreated by him. My mother had just stood by and watched. She did not even come to comfort me. My entire emotional system had broken down, and I was in distress. Why wouldn't she come? She saw how unjustly treated I felt, didn't she? My only answer was that she must not love me.

"I remember hearing 'Mommy doesn't love me, Mommy doesn't love me' over and over in my head. I started saying it out loud as I rocked on the bed trying to soothe myself.

"I vaguely heard someone coming up the stairs, but I could not get out of the emotional distress I was in.

"It was my father. Apparently, my mother had asked him to come upstairs and apologize to me. She had seen. She had acted on my behalf. But as my father approached, he heard me crying, 'Mommy doesn't love me,' and immediately assumed I was saying that on purpose to manipulate my mother and make her feel bad. He believed that I thought it was her coming up the stairs, and I was saying that just to hurt her.

"When he entered the room, he lashed out at me verbally, falsely accusing me. My distress increased, as I was shamed and rejected.

"I am rejectable. That is my conclusion. I am not worth people taking the time to understand my perspective. I am not worth the benefit of the doubt. I deserve to be rejected."

The knot in my stomach doubles me over. This "lie" feels 100% true to my little 9-year-old self.

I sit with this feeling for a brief moment. Then I remember to invite Jesus' perspective into my darkness: "Jesus, what do You think about all of this?"

Light breaks forth.

"I see Him there in each memory between me and my offender. He is facing them and takes their attacks into Himself. It is like He is a shield protecting me. He says He did protect me from even worse happening. I see my dad lifting his hand to slap me, but Jesus was there to stay his hand and make him leave the room. He was there protecting me." His presence in my memories changes the feelings embedded there. The knot in my stomach begins to loosen.

"Jesus wants to take all of that pain from me and carry it on Himself. I see Him absorbing it into His body."

I begin to feel seen and protected, like a little sheep that was lost in the woods with wolves all around, but now has the Good Shepherd there to fight off the attacks. I watch in amazement as He fights for me. I am no longer curled up in a ball. I have relaxed, and I sense tension leaving my shoulders.

After the defending is done, He turns toward me and holds out His hands. He invites me to give Him my pain and to stop trying to use it to protect myself.

"You mean I can't remain the victim here?" I sense a part of me wants to stay wounded and continue to shut others out, continue to believe that I am the only one who can protect me.

Looking straight into my eyes, He declares His truth to the kingdom of darkness and to the darkness in my very soul: "Toni, you are My precious, and you are worth being protected."

I am stunned. Where I believed I am shameful and deserve to be rejected, He declares I am precious and worth being protected.

It is not about what I deserve or do not deserve. It is about what I am worth, and He believes I am worth a great deal. He believes we all are worth His very life, even when we were still in darkness. He is my knight in shining armor, my Prince, my King. He has come to my rescue.

I want to let go. I open my hands face up and release the pain, the anger, the desire to protect. I trust. I remember the verse in Isaiah – "in quietness and trust is your strength," not in striving, fighting, defending, and shutting others out.

"Also, Toni, when a believer hurts you, they hurt Me, and they ultimately hurt themselves because we are all part of the same body. The work you do to forgive, to reconcile, to restore is not just for yourself, but for My body."

I feel soothed, calmed, at peace.

June takes me back to each memory that has surfaced. "What do you feel now?" she asks with each one.

These memories bring no more pain. I remember them, and I feel protected and worth being understood. My intent *does* matter. My identity is not in how I impact others, or what they think of me, or what I "deserve." I am precious and worth protecting no matter what.

I feel capable now of explaining myself to others without needing them to "get me." I understand that I will at times have misunderstandings with others based on their interpretations and my inability to explain myself well. However, if I consider myself precious and worth protecting, I can give myself to the process of explaining me and inquiring about them, knowing He is here holding me, protecting me. He sees my heart even when others do not. He knows my intentions. I know I am His precious one, and He will protect me.

April 21, 2006 – Healing Conversation

I was able to have a conversation with the women in the small group about this whole situation. All came to light. They admitted that they were negatively interpreting me, and that they were wrong in their attitude to make decisions out of fear instead of being willing and open to listen to Jesus together.

I cried a ton. It was a healing experience for me to be able to lovingly stand up for myself and invite others to own their own emotional dysfunction. It was one of the hardest things I have ever had to do. Our leader, Ann, could even own that she freezes when conflict happens, and that maybe, this is a pattern she needs to look at with a therapist.

This maturing work takes a ton of time and energy, but the results I am seeing make it so worth the journey. I am beginning to enjoy and value being me for the first time in my life!

September 2006 – Set Free

Father, a few days ago, I had this **wonderful** day. Better than EVER! I felt happy to be me, satisfied with who I am becoming in my relationships, thankful for my community, for the hard work of maturing, and for the amazing healing you have brought about in my life. It was so strange to be so happy. I have to say it is not my norm. I normally feel sad, stressed, pressed, and never able to do enough to relieve the pressure.

But *this* wonderful day was totally different. It was like sunshine breaking through the dark clouds. No, it was like flying above the clouds where the sun shines always. I felt free, and I wanted to celebrate, radically celebrate who You are and what You have done in my life. I felt Psalm 30:11, "You have turned for me my mourning into dancing; you have loosed my sack cloth and clothed me with gladness, that my glory may sing your praise and not be silent. Oh Lord, my God, I will give thanks to you forever!"

Stories from the Bible come to mind of what Your people have done when You have worked on their behalf in amazing ways. They would sometimes construct an altar to remind themselves that You were there for them, that You rescued them, that You healed them. The story of Joshua comes to mind when he led Your people across the Jordan River on dry ground (Joshua 4). You instructed them to take twelve stones from the middle of the dry riverbank and, once safe on the other side, they were to stack them as a memorial. "When your children ask their fathers in times to come, 'What do these stones mean?' then you shall let your children know, 'Israel passed over this Jordan on dry ground.' For the LORD your God dried up the waters of the Jordan for you until you passed over, as the LORD your God did to the Red Sea, which he dried up for us until we passed over, so that all the peoples of the earth may know that the hand of the LORD is mighty, that you may fear the LORD your God forever" (vs. 21-24).

I am being set free. I sense You working in my life in such an incredible way that I feel obligated to set up my stones of remembrance. I want to remind myself that You are radical: radical in Your love, radical in Your grace. I want to remember that Your Kingdom really has come and that freedom is here, now. I want to do something prophetic that announces Your joy to the world. I want it to symbolize the healing, community, and maturity that have led me to feel a glimpse of wholeness for the first time in my life. I want to mark the beginning of me entering into my promised land, the land of peace, rest, and joy that You died for and promised to me and to all who turn to You.

Dreadlocks come to mind. I know that is crazy and would rock the upper class, appearance-oriented little world that I live in here in Uruguay. I do not want to offend people. That is not my intention. I want to invite them into freedom.

The more I think about it, the more I see how dreadlocks are the perfect memorial. It is practically a joy-filled party on my head, which would represent the deep inner healing I am experiencing coming from God's enjoyment of me. Then, my friends and family can actually come make the dreads. They will all look different and slightly messy (like community), but beautiful when all together!

Lastly, they will have to mature. Dreadlocks are not easily formed on thin, straight hair like mine. I will have to work every day for years to get them to mature. It is a physical reminder to me that the work of emotional maturity is hard work that never stops. It will remind me that each of us has to do our own maturity work, in our own time and way, and that when we stay in relationship as we mature, it might be a mess at times, but is a beautiful, life-giving mess.

I want to listen to You, Papa. This is radical, and I do not go into this lightly. I know some will be impacted in a very negative way by looking at me. My appearance could possibly trigger feelings of disgust, but if they care to ask why I have them, I will have a chance to share Your amazing work in my life.

I hear the question, "Why not just let your life and love be radical? Why do you have to change your appearance?"

I want to be marked with a reminder that this world cannot and will not control me, that I have radically given myself to my God.

I sense Jesus smile and embrace me. I sense the words, "I did not fit into a box either, My child. Your prophetic tendencies come from me."

I will share with my community all that is stirring. I will wait at least 6 months to discern if this is really You or just me. I love You, my Good Shepherd.

Psalm 44 comes to mind. I want to play with You today and let you show me in my imagination what this looks like for me. Here it all is through my own "eyes":

> *I have heard with my own ears, O God, my parents have told me*
> *What You have done in their days and in mine.*
> *With Your own hand You drove the enemy away and saved my parents' lives and marriage.*
> *You tore down the strongholds of adultery and divorce and made my life flourish.*
> *It was not by their goodness or strength that they were saved*
> *But by Your gracious hand, Your right arm.*
> *You were a refuge and a shield to my family.*

You protected me with Your own two hands. And the light
of Your face has burned away shame, for You love us.
When the bondage of sexual impurity sought me out, You
intervened and rescued me time after time. You protected
me like a Father protects His daughter.
Your authority and power go before You to break the
chains.
You are my King and my God
Who proclaims victory for Your people.
Through You we push back our enemies.
Through Your name we trample our foes.

We walk in the victory You are accomplishing here in Uruguay. Proclaim it, and we will walk in it. Through You we defeat depression, unbelief, discouragement, and self-deception.

I do not trust in my spirituality, nor my discipline, nor my gifts. For I am an ant in the presence of my enemy, my gifts do not bring me victory.

But You give us victory, You put our enemies to shame, You give us strength to stand and not fear.

In God I set my hope, and I brag on Him all day long. I will praise Your name forever.

CHAPTER 6

For Personal Reflection and Practice

Jeff Van Vonderen, a pastor and psychologist who did an amazing video series titled *Wounded by Shame, Healed by Grace* says, "a shame-based system gets healthy one person at a time." I experienced this as true with this group of women I was meeting with. As I did *my* hard work of facing *my* own issues, I could move into relationship with them in a way that was compassionate, yet challenging to unhealthy interactions. As a result, the whole system got healthier. This does not always happen, unfortunately. Sometimes the people within the system do not want to grow or change, and they shame you even more to shut you up. This is subtle abuse and is addressed brilliantly in Jeff VanVonderen's work on *The Subtle Power of Spiritual Abuse.*

1. Go to an appreciation memory. Again, explore the physical and emotional sensations. Try to sense God's presence there with you in that memory. While you are in that memory take some time and explore the following questions.

- What unhealthy system, if any, am I currently a part of? How am I being challenged to grow by being a part of this community?

- Do I *feel* valuable to God? (Many of us have been told over and over again that we are "worthless" because we are so "unworthy". This is *far* from the truth. While we may be unworthy of God's love, we are so valuable to Him and worth His very life. If we were such worthless trash, God would have been incredibly stupid to pay such a high price for us. He apparently knows something about us, that we do not realize about ourselves, that would impel Him to die in order to save us.) If you do not *feel* valuable to Him, ask Him what that is about and spend some time listening.

If you are still struggling to sense God with you in appreciation memories or sense His voice speaking to you, I suggest you watch this video by Mark Virkler (www.youtube.com/watch?v=8czdKN4U0hc). Also, pick up the book *Joyful Journey: Listening to Immanuel* by E. James Wilder, Anna Kang, John Loppnow, and Sungshim Loppnow. *Hearing God* and *Renovation of the Heart* by Dallas Willard are also helpful if you are looking for a more theological basis for this type of contemplative work. If, after practicing the exercises therein you are still struggling, you might consider finding a coach who is experienced in sensing God's presence and helping other's do the same.

2. Has God moved in your life in such a way that you need to construct a memorial? If so, ask God what kind of memorial you need to make. What is the story that needs to be remembered and retold for the generations to come?

Pride, It Finally Makes Sense

October 2006 – Show Me More

Pride. I have sensed it within me all of my life. I have journal entries from when I was 12 years old begging God to rid me of my pride, this attitude that I am better than others. It is such a strange bird, too, because I know that deep down I am scared to death of being rejected, left alone, or abandoned. Pride and Fear. This all makes no sense to me.

At present, I am struggling greatly in my relationship with Matt, both as a wife and as a coworker. Personally, it seems that when I need him the most, he is not available. And in a work context, he tends to not be reliable either. I have to hound him in order for him to get one thing done. He forgets to call people, he double schedules himself, he avoids people, and I am struggling with how to handle this in a compassionate yet professional way.

I am also struggling to trust God when I am counseling others. I trust Him to be there for me when I need Him, but will He really be there for others? I don't deserve for Him to heal someone else, and I don't deserve to be a part of something so incredible. I am afraid He will not come, afraid we won't get past the barriers, afraid I won't know how to get someone unstuck, and afraid that He won't come for them. It feels out of control, nervous, and scary.

My personal counseling session yesterday was weird. Things were revealed, but I did not see You, Jesus, or even sense You. I felt like I was alone trying to figure it all out, and yet it was too big for me to deal with by myself. There was a lot of pain. I could not get back to where the memories began or to where the pain began.

What I did discover was that my prideful attitude, the "I can do it better than others" attitude, was apparently once my friend and protected me from the emotionally hostile environment I sometimes found myself in. I would like to know more about this, Papa. Please lead the way.

November 2006 – Letting Him Enjoy Me

"I feel pride right here with me. I can't trust others with things that are precious to me. Whether they are people, objects, or tasks, if I trust others with them, they will get broken or left undone. If I want something done right, I have to do it myself." I come right out the corner fighting today in my counseling session, lies already on the surface.

"How does that make you feel?" Linda asks, my friend and co-worker who has lovingly agreed to help me process today.

"It is not fair!" I respond hopelessly. "I can't do everything for everyone!"

I am feeling alone, nervous, scared, and small. Very small.

People are leaving me again. It is the nature of our life here in Uruguay. People come and they go. That is unfair, as well. I want to shut down, not say goodbye. I cannot handle the sadness anymore.

"Do you see Jesus there?" Linda probes.

"No. There is nothing here. I am in a dark closet all alone with no hope. I know I cannot solve this. I know it is beyond me. And I also know that if Jesus does not show up, I will be here forever lost in darkness. He is my only hope, but will He come for me?"

The image changes and I am all curled up, very, very small, and surrounded by black space. This feels so hopeless. I am alone, in deep, dark space with no hope of return.

"Can you ask Jesus if there are any memories related to these feelings? Why are you alone?" Linda guides the process.

Memories surface of times when I would get in trouble when I was a child, yet I did not know what I had done wrong. In some of these instances, I know I clearly had done nothing wrong. I was just being a child who had needs, but my caregiver was angry and treated me unfairly out of their own inability to handle their emotions. I rarely felt listened to or understood.

Then there was a memory where I pitched a fit of some sort and cried myself to sleep on the hallway floor. Why didn't someone come and at least put me to bed? Why was I alone there? I'm sure they thought I just needed to get the fit out of my system, but I feel like I needed someone to BE with me in my sadness. To help me know I was not alone. To tell me it would be alright. To help me understand my emotions.

More memories come, and what I see is hard to acknowledge because it demands a new level of maturity, a maturity that understands the complexities of the human soul. I know my parents loved me deeply. I know they would have done anything for me. And I know they did the best they could with what they had. I love them, honor them, respect them, and am so thankful to God for them.

But that doesn't negate the reality that some things that happened to me were hurtful or damaging to my identity. Somehow I feel invited by God to grieve what was lost in my family. Somehow this is necessary for my healing. I am willing to see what was lost.

I see for the first time that as much as my parents loved me and did their absolute best to raise us, I grew up in emotional confusion. My environment was unpredictable. I lived in fear of never knowing when I would get in trouble or when I would be enjoyed. I felt emotionally unsafe, like no one could help me sort through all of the strong feelings I was feeling, let alone feel them with me and help me get back to joy. Many times my emotions were invalidated, made fun of, and ignored. And my true heart was not seen or encouraged to grow.

Because of my fear of rejection, I tried to live perfectly, be the prettiest, the most popular, the most successful, the most godly. But the crazy-making part of that is that no matter how hard I tried, I always messed up anyway.

This plight felt hopeless. Try hard; get in trouble anyway. I felt like I could never please and never be good enough.

"What lies do you hear in these memories?" Linda probes as I share some of what I am seeing.

I hear, "You cannot trust. As soon as you think it is safe, you will be hit. As soon as you open your heart, people will make fun of you."

"But I didn't want to shut my heart down," I add. "I did not want to close myself off to my family. I loved them, and I knew that they loved me."

"So, how did you respond?" my guide continues.

"I see myself at the refrigerator door. I had just dropped a jar of pickles. My dad is chastising me, calling me clumsy, accusing me of not paying attention. And then, I see it happen, something within me stands straight up and pushes back. Inside my head, I hear the words, 'I am NOT stupid. I am smart! Don't listen to him. You are better than he says you are. You don't deserve to be treated like this!'

"Pride, it was like a secret weapon that formed inside me to combat the shame that was attacking me. It also kept me from feeling the sadness and anger that I probably should have felt. I did not know what to do with those emotions at the time. Pride became my friend and my defense mechanism."

"How does that make you feel?" the questions continue.

"Sad. I am sad that I had to do that in order to keep my heart open. I am sad that parts of me did not feel appreciated or enjoyed by my own family. I know they tried to enjoy me, but for some reason right now, all I feel is torn down and isolated. Jesus, is it wrong to appreciate myself or be proud of myself?"

Jesus is there in my memory in the kitchen with me. He takes the pickle jar out of my hands, bends down to my level, and looks into my little face. As I stare into His eyes, I begin to feel something almost foreign to my soul. He is enjoying me, even though I dropped the pickle jar. He is there enjoying me in my shame. He appreciates my heart.

"I want you to feel MY appreciation over you. That is what matters! It is okay that you break things, that you are not perfect. I love you as broken as you are. You are still so valuable to Me!"

Jesus all of a sudden looks like a shepherd and we are transported to a field and I am one lamb in the midst of one hundred. He comes over and picks me up and takes me away from the other sheep to be alone with me. He sits me down and takes time to just enjoy me. I want to dance around and play. It feels so awkward for someone to give me attention like this. I have not had my heart this open for anyone to enjoy for a long time now. I sense my soul shifting from deep within.

"What do I do about the prideful part of me?" I ask Jesus.

"Let it go, My child. You do not need it anymore!" He responds.

This seems too easy to be true. But I hold out my hands, I thank the pride for protecting me as a child, and I release it from its duty. "We do not need you anymore, He will enjoy us!" I am not sure it is gone for good, but at least it has been fired from its job!

"But, Papa, what does all of this have to do with people letting me down? I feel so tired," I ask curiously.

"As you experience My compassion over you, you will learn to have compassion for yourself and for others," Jesus answers.

"Yes, but if I have compassion on others, won't I get mistreated? Just take cleaning my house, for example. I hate cleaning up after everyone, but it seems like if I don't do all of the work, I will live in a dump! I am so tired of doing all of the work. So I bark at my family and shame them to try to get them to clean. What would compassion on them look like? I don't want to make them afraid of me like I was afraid of my father, but I don't know what to do! I feel so presumed upon!"

Memories come of my dad griping about the house being cluttered with our stuff everywhere. I realize what hurt so badly is that he seemed to care more about the house being cleaned than about his relationship with me.

"I am not important," I say definitively.

"What do you mean?" says Linda.

"That is what is getting triggered here. I am not important. I do not feel important to my father. I know I was, but at this moment, I do not FEEL like I was."

I begin crying again. Where does all the pain come from, I wonder. It seems like there is a bottomless well filled with it.

I return to the image of me, a lamb, with the Good Shepherd. He picks me up and begins to hold me like a baby and gaze into my eyes. All of a sudden, I become a newborn baby, and Jesus is holding me, cherishing me, enjoying me.

"Don't you have things to do?" I ask Him, feeling very vulnerable and tentative.

"No. There is nothing more important right now than being with you and enjoying you. You are important to Me!"

The circuitry in my brain is being rewired as I let Him enjoy me. Who could have ever helped me see that the Christian life is about **letting Him enjoy me**? I was always taught that it was about ME loving Him, ME worshiping Him, ME seeking Him, ME trying to get to know Him, ME serving Him, ME giving Him praise, honor, etc. It seemed to always start with ME. But this starts with Him, Him creating, Him seeking, Him finding, Him making time for, Him enjoying, Him healing. This is all new. I wonder if this is what born again means, letting myself receive from Him like a baby receives from its parents? This is not about *doing* anything, but about letting Him do for me, letting Him meet the needs of my soul, letting Him enjoy me, letting Him be proud of me!

A few minutes pass, and I am transported to where we began this session, back to me curled up and small and all alone in the middle of a black space.

"Are you still feeling lonely, scared, and hopeless?" Linda asks.

"No, not at all. It is strange, but it actually feels like a womb now, and there is nothing hopeless or lonely about it. I feel comforted and peaceful." As air fills my lungs, my whole body relaxes. Peace enters every cell throughout my body all the way to my limbs.

My mind cannot get around the implications of what has just happened. "What does all of this mean?" I ask Jesus for clarification.

"I knew you before you were born, Toni. The darkness was light to me. I created your inmost being; I knit you together in your mother's womb. You are fearfully and wonderfully made. Your frame was not hidden from me when you were made in the secret place, when you were woven together in the depths of the earth; my eyes saw your unformed body. I began enjoying you even back then in the darkness of the womb."

I had heard Psalm 139 so many times, but never before had I felt what David must have been feeling when he wrote it!

With His intense enjoyment of me, my sadness surfaces again. "Oh, Papa, what do I do with the sadness that I feel for all that has happened to me, for all that has been lost?"

"I want you to feel it. My presence will give you strength. I want your grief to motivate you to create a safe place where children can come and be seen, a place that is emotionally healthy and safe. You will forever know the power of attuning with children and meeting them where they are emotionally. I will use this passion and ability in you to mentor and to create safe places for adults, as well."

Godly Play. Last year, I had been exposed to a very different kind of Christian education for children that change the way I understood kid's ministry. This way of being with children actually fed me, challenged me and helped me draw near to God. I remember telling Jesus that if He would let me take Godly Play to Uruguay, I would give my life for that purpose. It is a methodology that is based on relational skills, emotional health, and contemplative Christianity. It is also perfect for multigenerational community and house churches. Now I see why I had been so drawn to it.

"Thank you, Papa, for redeeming ALL that was lost!" I stay in that safe, black space. I see myself as a newborn, and He is holding me and enjoying me. I see myself as the little lamb, and He is proud of me. I feel important and valuable.

My problems are not solved, but they do not matter. The pride finally makes sense now, why it has been with me for so long. I feel a stillness inside that makes it easier to see what is really going on in my relationships in the present. I can see now how I can let go of some things that bother me in order to focus on the importance of the people in my life, not so much the outward appearance of things. Also, I can ask for my needs to be met because I am important enough to have my needs met, too. I feel free to engage differently with relational situations, and I see ways forward that I did not see before.

CHAPTER 7

For Personal Reflection and Practice

"Compassion for weakness" is a catchphrase in the Life Model Works/Joy Starts Here community. In Joy Starts Here, the authors state that in order for joy to transform our communities there must be three conditions in place: The "weak and the strong" are together; compassion for weakness or "tender responses to weakness" is normative; and the interactive sensing God's presence which brings about peace or "shalom" (pg. 52).

My pride made me appear strong on the outside. At times I came off as judgmental and arrogant. But, in reality I was the weak one! I was using pride to mask that I felt unimportant and rejectable. It is so hard to have compassion on others' weaknesses when we do not have compassion for our own.

1. How do you relate to yourself when you mess up or do something wrong? Do you beat yourself up, shame yourself, make excuses for yourself? Or, can you feel God's compassion on you and therefore, feel compassion for yourself, forgive yourself and make it right?

2. How do you relate to others when they mess up? Do you become impatient, angry, and judgmental? If so, then you probably treat yourself the same way. For me, the road to having more compassion on myself and others has been to watch Jesus as He responds to me when I mess up. Go back and read this chapter and watch how the "Good Shepherd" gently responds to my weakness. Follow your heart in journaling about how this impacts you.

3. Do you take time to let God enjoy you? If not, ask yourself and Jesus what that would look like for you? For some, it is participating in creating something, running, walking in the woods or on the beach. For others, it is in the laughter and eyes of a friend. For still others, it is in the silence of their imagination. Whatever the situation may be, all of it involves an awareness of His presence there with you, enjoying you. Does this even feel possible to you that the God of the Universe wants to enjoy you?! Let God know what you are thinking and ask Him what He thinks about all of this.

I am Not a Powerless Victim

December 2007 – Enjoying Others

"This whole year has felt violent against my soul on all fronts, and I am downright angry. However, I do not want to hurt with my anger, so I close up inside, detach from others and go numb." I begin our counseling session today with raw honesty.

"But I hate being numb because it not only numbs the pain, but the joy, as well. And when I do this, I cannot sense God with me. I just feel, well, numb."

"Can you tell me what else you are feeling?" My counselor begins her probing questions.

"My teammates have taken responsibilities away from me without explaining what is going on. I know some of them are assuming my motives for actions I take. Then, they make these decisions based on their assumptions. But I believe their assumptions are wrong. They don't see the need to try to clarify my motives, nor to have a real conversation with me about any of this. It seems like these types of interactions happen so often on this team!

"I see how they get triggered, how they shut down, how they lash out. Yet they only see themselves as right and me as the one with issues. I spend hours trying to process my own stuff, so that I can respond well without hurting them, and yet I get blamed for everything."

"Yes, and how does that make you feel?" she presses.

"Angry, avoided, excluded, feared, defenseless, misunderstood. I feel like it is my lot in life to suffer because others won't face their emotional issues! It is unfair, and I feel all alone in this."

"Are there any memories associated with the feelings?" Even before the words leave the counselor's mouth, I see images in my mind from my past.

"A really bad fight with my dad. A porn video my older cousins thought would be funny to show me. The two boys that trapped me in their house and pestered me until I jumped off of the two story balcony, breaking my right leg in three places." I list them and briefly explain each one.

"What do all of these memories have in common?" the counselor prompts.

"I feel defenseless and angry. I am left alone to pick up the pieces of other people's brokenness. I can't defend myself no matter how hard I try. People will always be able to hurt me. There is nothing I can do about it.

"And somehow they seem happy living in their dysfunction and their lies. Their way seems much less painful than mine. They seem fine, and I am a mess. I am tired of feeling pain because they don't do their maturity work."

It is hard to be honest. The intellectual part of my brain knows that these attitudes are not "Christian." But I am learning to be honest with what I am feeling. Jesus can handle even the ugly inside of me.

As these thoughts become audible words, I hear alongside of them other thoughts forming. I wonder if I am sensing Jesus' thoughts. I turn the volume up and speak out loud what I am hearing. "If you face your painful past, the present pain will not hurt as badly."

So, the present must be triggering more stuff from my past, making my present emotions feel two or three times stronger than they should feel.

My soul surrenders to this truth, and I let myself drift to the past. I feel myself in a closet where I once hid as a teenager. I feel helpless and alone. I had had a fight with my dad. I don't remember the details, but I remember being so hurt that I ran out of the room and straight to my closet to hide. I was trying to get safe. The words "I can't stop them, I can't stop them" repeat over and over again in my mind. I am crying and rocking back and forth in the counselor's office.

"Where are You, Jesus?" My mind is trained to look for Him now.

Truth comes like a soft breeze into my thoughts, and with the words, I sense Jesus there. "Toni, you DID do something to stop them. You called out to Me that night! That was all you needed to do. Do you remember what happened after that?"

"I do. My mom came to comfort me. Then my sister came and apologized, I think she had something to do with the fight." Remembering their hugs brings a smile to my face. They had sought me out.

Then, I remember the miracle that had occurred later on. "My dad had come and apologized to me. I was already in bed by that time about to go to sleep. He came in, sat next to my bed, and for the first time that I can remember, he humbled himself, apologized to me, and asked me to forgive him!"

Remembering this moment brings thankfulness to my soul. It was, indeed, a major shift in my relationship with my dad. He earned more respect that night than he had my whole life. And with his apology, my healing process began.

"I did that!" Jesus stands in my memory and tilts His chin toward my dad on the couch. "As a result of your prayers that night, I moved in his heart to apologize to you, and he obeyed. I

99

was so satisfied when I saw him say those words, and your little heart found healing. I knew it was only the beginning of the restoration you would find on your journey."

"What about my co-workers? What does all of this have to do with them?" I ask, curious as to how this is all linked together.

"Those who hurt you *do* suffer the consequences in their relationships. They might not let themselves feel their pain, but it is there, destroying them. I was there in the closet with you, and I am here now. I want you to rest and not defend yourself against them."

As He speaks these words, I am only partially understanding them, but I feel deeply understood by Him.

Somehow it is like He is calling me out of a victim mentality, this attitude that I am helpless when others hurt me, that there is nothing I can do to stop people from taking things from me that I have not given.

This new way of seeing things feels very foggy, but His reality is so inviting. I want to give up my anger, but the 17-year-old inside of me cries out, "I don't want to be left picking up the pieces when others do a crappy job or break things because of their lack of personal growth and maturity!"

"As I heal you, My child, you will not have to pick the pieces up. You will not get as triggered emotionally, and you will have new skills to be able to invite others into a different reality. You will have more options of how to respond to others.

"Part of this requires you to stop wanting people to be different than they are. Can you enjoy them instead?"

I picture my dad. In my mind, I see him insulting people for thinking the way they do, watching tons of TV instead of engaging with us emotionally, and yelling at us for normal childlike behavior. But I also see him laughing, giving his time to fix my car, spending hours coaching my softball teams, eating dinner with us every night around the table, creating belonging with my friends by taking the risk of initiating a board game or a night of karaoke.

I laugh out loud. "Yes," I mutter between laughter. "Yes, I can enjoy my dad." There is a very real shift in me that takes place. I can see my dad's strengths. I can enjoy those strengths, and I can have compassion on his weaknesses. Because Papa God is meeting my emotional needs, I don't NEED my dad to meet them. I can accept him as he is, love him as he is, and invite him into a deeper, healthier relationship if he wants that. However, my growth and development does not depend on him getting help or wanting to go deeper with me. "I can enjoy him," I conclude, "I am not a helpless victim!"

CHAPTER 8

For Personal Reflection and Practice

1. Do you feel like the victim sometimes in unfair situations? Do you feel like there is nothing you can do to stop someone from hurting you? For me, this was an invitation to dig deeper, to own my own emotions (including my anger) and to get help processing them. Some emotional difficulties are too big to conquer on your own, especially if you are in an abusive relationship or in a relationship with an addict, or in a shame based system. If this is you, I encourage you to get professional counseling as well as find an inner healing practitioner that can help you navigate through what you do have control over, versus what you do not have control over. Both Theophostic Prayer Ministry as well as the Immanuel Approach have directories you can search to try and find someone close to you.

2. Is there a person in your life who currently "bothers" you? How would things change if you asked God for the grace to enjoy that person? What would enjoying them look like? Can you visualize enjoying them in your mind?

Imaginative Play in Prayer

2008 – Let It Go

In my quiet times of late, I have been drawn to sit with God in my imagination and ask Him to lead me where I need to go. Sometimes I am drawn to song, sometimes to stories or verses from the Bible. It is always a little unnerving because I am not in control of our time together. Following some sort of plan every day, while great at times, tends to give me a sense of control over our relationship. The truth is that I am not in control, nor should I be. So today I enter again into the unknown, and I ask my Creator to lead me where He knows I need to go...

I quiet myself and close my eyes... In my imagination, I hear the song, "You are Beautiful Beyond Description" being sung by hundreds, maybe thousands of people. I open my eyes in my imagination, and I am at a celebration in honor of the King! The streets are filled with people. The courtyard is overflowing. It reminds me of the scene out of *Lord of the Rings: Return of the King* when Aragorn is finally crowned. It is breathtaking, and I am caught up in the moment. There is great joy in the land. Our King is good. He cares for us. He loves us. His power is extensive, His beauty, breathtaking.

And I am there. It is a holy moment... filled with so much joy. Slowly, however, I notice sadness coming over me, and I find myself crying. I don't even know why. A twinge of shame runs through my body as I think, "What is wrong with me, NOW?" I tend to be oversensitive, or at least that is what I have been told; so, why am I crying now, at this happy celebration?

As I weep, I look up at the King and freeze. His eyes meet mine. My King sees me. The King sees ME. Among thousands of smiles and laughter, somehow, He notices me... crying. I try to hide behind the crowd, but to no avail. He sees me anyway.

He gets up off His throne, steps off of the stage, and begins parting the people to get to me. My heart pounds within my chest. I tell myself to stop crying, but there is nothing I can do to stop the tears.

"Why are you sad, My child?" He says as He gently takes my shoulders in His hands, almost lifting me off the ground.

"I do not know, my King," I reply, weeping all the more. His "seeing" me somehow releases unknown pain from deep within.

"What is troubling your heart on such a glorious day when there is so much joy?" He tries to make eye contact with me. As I let myself be seen, His eyes enter into my pain.

"My Lord, my King. While Your Kingdom is so great and grand and extensive, there is still so much that does not yield itself to Your hand, so much in me, in others around me, and in the world. I fear, my King. I am weighted down with fear, and I do not know how to surrender it. I still feel so immature as a person, so inadequate to face all the brokenness in the world."

I can hardly believe the confession that is coming out of my mouth. From somewhere beyond the conscious level of awareness, a part of me is speaking which I do not know all that well myself.

He gently takes my face in His hands and kisses my cheek... then my neck... and then I fall into His embrace, heaving with tears. He envelops me. He is not repulsed by my fear or my immaturity. He feels so much compassion for me.

He picks me up and carries me back to His throne to be with Him. He asks no more questions. He does not badger me. "Just sit with Me awhile," He says. "Let me enjoy you. My enjoyment of you will melt your fears, My child... whatever they may be. Rest with me awhile."

As He enjoys looking at me, just sitting with me, I see that He really expects nothing from me. The weight of His love brings more tears as waves of emotion come and go over me. My present becomes mixed with my imagination.

"What about the rent?" I ask.

"Just let it go." His eyes are inviting.

"What about the school fees?" I hand Him another problem.

"Just let it go."

"What about the money for the tickets to the US?" I am insistent.

"Just let it go."

I obviously am not getting the point, "What about..."

"Just let it go," He cuts me off firmly but lovingly. "Just let Me enjoy you right now."

Silence.

I can't. The tears flow even harder, and I almost feel nauseated. "How... can You... enjoy THIS?" I ask referring to myself. "This ball of sadness, fear, and messed-upness?" I am so aware of my brokenness. I am impatient with my children. I still get life out of looking good on the outside. I still disrespect my husband at times and snap at others when they are slow to understand.

"You just don't know the whole story, My child," He calmly responds. He knows something about me that I do not know. Something that helps Him see me differently, with grace and compassion... part of my story that explains why I am the way I am.

"I am afraid of messing up. Doing something wrong. Hurting my children or others because of my own immaturity or inability to bring them to You." There it is... a hidden fear that has been controlling my actions for years, weighing me down, making me tired, clouding my judgment. I live in fear of getting it wrong.

While the tears flow, it feels good to get everything out in the open, out of the darkness. It also feels good to have someone inside the brokenness with me.

Silence.

"Papa," I continue, "the evil in this world is too great for me to fight."

"The evil in this world has been broken, My child. It has suffered a fatal wound," He says so matter-of-factly with a victorious glint in His eyes.

"But I feel it, Jesus. I feel the evil all around me."

He looks directly into me with an intensity that begs my full attention. "Do you feel My love, child?"

"Yes, Papa. I do," I say, almost surprising myself. You see, for many years I could not feel His love. Maybe parts of me could, but not the hidden parts. His love was something I sung about, and read about, but it would not begin to penetrate me until I was almost 30 years old, just five years ago.

"Do you feel My compassion for you?" He continues.

"Oh, yes, Papa, I do," I respond with a smile as the recent memory of Him whisking me off my feet fills my heart.

His next words are measured, slow, and powerful. "You... are... a... beautiful... creation... Toni."

Silence.

Wrapped in His love and compassion, I stare into His eyes. "Does He really mean that?" I think to myself, searching for non-verbal evidence, micro expressions that might give Him away. It settles in. He really believes that I am a beautiful creation.

The crying finally stops, and the weight of His declaration over me brings peace. There is a calmness that moves in and takes me over. The questions are still there. Where should our oldest go to school next year? Will we be able to afford our youngest starting school? How do we buy tickets to the US without money?

Will we have to move AGAIN?

But for now, the fear of getting it wrong or hurting someone seems to have melted away. I lean my head on His lap and fall asleep. I am tired. "Thank You, Papa, for seeing me today..." I mumble as I drift off in my imagination. "Thank You for noticing me in a sea of faces. Thank You for being glad to be with me even when I am afraid and ashamed."

I open my eyes, and while I can still feel the tiredness, I am also energized. A huge weight, that I did not even know was there, has been lifted. A smile comes across my face and I go into my world lighter. I don't have to have all of the answers to be loved. I don't have to fear getting it wrong. I can rest in Him and be more present to enjoy myself and my family.

CHAPTER 9

For Personal Reflection and Practice

1. How does it feel to think about spending un-structured time with God, time where you have not set the agenda? Journal about how that would feel for you.

2. Go to an "interactive appreciation" memory, one of your memories where you feel full of appreciation and possibly where you sense God there. Remember to ask yourself how you feel physically and emotionally. Then, ask God how He would like to spend your time together. See if you can sense what He would like to do with you. Be open to anything. He can be so outside of the box. I have sensed Him wanting to jump on the trampoline together, dance together, take a long walk on the beach, go to a café for coffee, take a nap together, and yes, at times read the Bible. He knows what I need more than I do. Sometimes he surprises me by asking me what I want to do with Him, so be ready to start dialoguing.

3. Share your experience with at least two other people.

CHAPTER 10

Perfect Peace Moves In

February 22, 2010 – Under My Care

It was midnight. I was alone in a cab on the way to the hospital. Something was wrong, and my unborn son was trying to come three months early! The contractions had been going on for several hours. They must have been brought on by the dehydration I had been suffering that day. At least, that is what I thought.

It had all been a whirlwind – arriving back in Uruguay, staying out at the retreat center while we prepared a house to move into, leading a retreat for our community, moving into our new home, all within 30 days' time. We had just celebrated my birthday with our friends, but I had felt sick all day. It didn't seem like anything serious, just fatigue. I assumed that was normal. This was my third pregnancy, after all, and I am 37!

After the events of the day yesterday, I finally laid down to sleep, and in the stillness realized I was having contractions! Thinking back throughout the day, I was horrified to admit they had been coming for six hours now! I left our two other kids with Matt and took a taxi (yes, a taxi!) to the hospital, completely unaware of the seriousness of the situation.

As the taxi drove down the coastal highway, out of the blue, an image came to me so vividly that it felt real. In the image, I was there, pregnant and lying down in the palm of a large hand that was cuddled around me. It was God's hand, and I was cradled in it, safe and sound.

I focused on the image until nothing else was in my mind. My body relaxed all over, and I felt a peace radiate from within me. It was beyond words. It was not something I conjured up, coerced, or brainwashed myself into. It was just there, unsolicited. Peace, calm, complete trust.

The words "You are not outside of My hands. You both are under My care" came to my mind, and I received them from God Himself. A smile came over my face as I rubbed the baby in my tummy and settled in for the ride.

Upon arriving at the hospital, I quickly realized the gravity of the situation. They said my water had broken, and I would not be able to leave the hospital until he was born. They immediately called my doctor to come in to assess the situation.

"Toni, I do not know what to do with you. This is a hard call. I either take the baby and risk his life to save you, or I leave the baby and risk losing you if the infection spreads."

Wow. I had no idea. I thought it was just dehydration and a little fatigue, but I must have had an infection without realizing it. Apparently, the infection had caused a slight fissure in the placenta.

There was a slight temptation to worry, but before I could even go there, the image of me being cared for by God Himself was so strong that I could not have been distressed even if I had tried. I was in complete and utter peace. I knew everything was going to be fine, no matter what happened. I looked at the doctor. I could see that she was terribly distressed.

"Are you okay, doc?" I asked.

"My father was just taken to the emergency room in critical condition. We don't know if he is going to make it," she vulnerably shared with me.

Her reaction started to make sense. A year earlier, I actually went into labor the day after her mother had passed away. She came back to work only to deliver my precious Anne. Unfortunately, I reminded her of her loss.

Now, a year later, her father was in critical condition and there I was in labor, again, but three months early. This couldn't be happening to her. She not only feared for her father's life, but now my baby's and mine as well.

My heart was filled with compassion for what she must have been going through. "Can I pray for you?" I said, sensing Papa God reaching out to her through my own body. She could not believe her eyes and ears. How could I be so calm? How could I be seeing her need instead of being wrapped up in my own emotional storm?

I asked God to give her wisdom on which decision to make regarding my baby and me, to comfort her heart, and to lead her into a trusting relationship with Himself. Afterward, I took her hand, looked into her eyes, and said with a certainty that could be felt deep within, "I fully believe that I am in the palm of God's hand right now. You make the decision without fear. I trust our God will guide you."

She pursed her lips together thinking for a moment and still holding my hands said, "We wait until tomorrow and hope the infection will be gone. That will give the baby's lungs some time to respond to the cortisone treatment. Ideally, we need three days…"

February 23, 2010 – No Fear

This afternoon, my doctor entered the room in complete relief. My blood was clean, no infection, no fear of losing my life! Amazed and relieved, she explained that we could safely wait until my body went into natural birth.

March 23, 2010 – Do Not Worry

Exactly three days after I entered the hospital, Matty, my beautiful gift from God, was born with his lungs working perfectly.

After the birth, when I was tempted to worry about him. The image in my mind changed, and I was in one hand of God, and Matty was in the other. I sensed the Lord say, "I will care for him in the incubator. You must care for yourself and be strong to face what is to come. But do not worry for him. He is going to be fine."

My body relaxed, a smile came across my face, and I was filled with gratitude that my Papa would give me such a precious gift in such a critical time of need, before I even knew I needed it.

A few weeks later, a close atheist friend of mine called me as she was facing a difficult delivery herself. "Toni," she began, "I have to tell you that I am amazed at how you got through the whole situation with Matty. Every time I talked to you, you were at peace. I would have been an emotional wreck! I don't know how you did it, but I want what you have! Can you tell me how you do it?"

I laughed in disbelief! The thought of me, the one who has been characterized by internal emotional overwhelm, now being accused of exuding peace from within. It is ludicrous! It is amazing! It is a peace I did not try to conjure up. It just came to me as a gift from my Creator, my Lover, my Friend.

CHAPTER 10

For Personal Reflection and Practice

1. Think back and ask yourself if you have ever felt God's peace come to you in a time of great need.
    *   Write your story down and share it with at least two other people. Remember to reflect on how you felt emotionally *and* physically before you sensed God as well as after you sensed God intervene. If not, go to an appreciation memory and enjoy His presence there.

    *   Thank God for His intervention in your life
    *   Ask Him if there is anything else you need to know about that memory. Write down your answers.
    *   Share your story with at least two people.

2. If you cannot think of a time like this, go to an appreciation memory and ask God if there was a time when he intervened that, perhaps, you are not aware of. Notice what you notice physically and emotionally. Write down your thoughts.

PART III

· · · · ·

Walking with Immanuel
(God with Us)
(2010-2012)

Daybreak

June 2009

I walk in it, this night
So natural, so known that I hardly notice it.
Deep, dark, terrorizing
And yet when the dawn breaks,
It unleashes a burst of hope, of freedom
That runs across the sky and envelops the darkness until it is no
more.

The light is a power so much bigger than myself
And so... not about me.
Almost terrifying, and yet there is comfort in its coming.
I can fail or succeed and regardless the sun will come
And the darkness will flee.
I can rest in this reality.

A Note Before You Continue

I believe that God approaches each of us with complete individuality. In this book, I describe experiences with God that relate to who I am as a female with my own personality and history in view. How you might experience intimacy with the Creator will most likely be entirely different based on who you are – male/female, younger/older, etc. If my experiences of God seem odd to you or make you feel uncomfortable, just remind yourself that your experiences of Him might have the same impact me. The point is that He is able to love each of us in the way we need Him to at each point in our journey with Him.

God with Me: Physical Experience of Spiritual Reality

October 2010 – Sparkles

I wake up early one morning and am led away to walk on the beach. "Stop thinking about all of the problems, and come be with Me," I hear. "Quiet your mind, and rest in My arms."

I wish it were easy, this quieting. Sometimes it just happens without effort, but even after years of practice, at times it still feels like a battle. I accept the invitation.

As I walk, I am amazed at the ocean, the beach, the seagulls. I breathe the fresh air deep into my lungs and feel the breeze on my arms. The worries quiet, and something magical begins to happen. The sky, pregnant with clouds, has a strange effect on the air around me. I stop, breathe, quiet my soul, become fully present with all of my senses, and all of a sudden I see them... little white dots glimmering and dancing all about me. Like little pin flashes of light, they are fluttering about as if to celebrate my life. It is as if they want to call attention to the fact that they are always there, always with me, surrounding me, flowing through me, these sparkles of life.

I reach out to touch them. "Am I going mad?" I think to myself. I am sure they are just air particles floating around that I usually only see in a sunbeam. But their presence profoundly shakes me: the closeness of God in even the smallest visible speck to the greatness of God in the vast sky and ocean.

The Spirit walks with me. For a moment, I imagine these specks gathering together in a semi solid form, and I can see outside of my body the "wind" or the "spirit" of God walking with me. I laugh out loud in delight. I smile from ear to ear. Stress shatters and falls off of my body like ice as it thaws and falls off of a tree.

This is straight out of a sci-fi movie, I know. My imagination has run amuck. But I feel the Spirit here. "Give me eyes that see the spiritual world, eyes that see reality the way You do, to see what is around us spiritually, the angels, the demons. Give me eyes to see You, all of You, in every sunset, in every wave, in every soul."

As I revel in this Presence, an old worship song about the Holy Spirit being the very air we breathe comes to mind. And so I breathe. Deeply.

I take this memory with me, and somehow feel like I have finally encountered the Holy Spirit in a way that I can sense and grasp. The Spirit is different than how I perceive the Father and the Son. The Spirit is other, beautiful, electric, in motion, glimmering, dancing, fluttering, shimmering, and powerful. I feel precious and strong, not because of who I am, but because I am beginning to believe Creator really does live within me.

October 2010 – Held

Heavy day today. I have been depressed for weeks now. Mourning not having my parents close by while my babies are so little.

Depleted from a five-day fever. I feel like I am inside myself. Where are you, soul?

I see myself small, like a baby, and held close to God's chest, like I was holding Matty yesterday. God takes my head in His hands and caresses His face against mine. He breathes in deeply, enjoying me, enjoying comforting me, enjoying being with me. Just like I am with my babies, He is with me.

My thoughts slow down. The sadness dissipates. My senses reach out to feel what is happening in my imagination. Could this be real? Could I actually feel God touching me even if I still cannot see Him with my physical eyes? I am fully present for the moment. I am at rest, at peace. I do not have to work all of my problems out right now. I do not have to fix other people's problems. I just have to rest, in You, and be who You have made me to be, showing up with all of me in each relationship I have.

Hold me, Papa. I will quit struggling so, and I will let You hold me and let You enjoy me. The load lightens, and I feel deeply enjoyed, and I am at peace.

January 2011 – Appreciation

Matt and I have decided to pursue more studies that have to do with the *Life Model* book. It turns out that they have a three-year relational skills-based leadership development training. We have jumped right into it. We are seeing that our family up until the last year has been characterized by tension and striving, not by being glad to be together. Our oldest is struggling to form healthy peer bonds, and we are at our end as to how to help.

The courses that we are taking online and through DVDs from Dr. Jim Wilder are revolutionary, not only for our own lives individually and as a family, but also for the emotional and spiritual health of our churches and leaders here in Uruguay.

One of the areas we are working on is sensing God's presence with us in the present. While I have encountered the Divine in so many ways in the past, it is still not a daily occurrence. It happens mostly when I am overwhelmed emotionally and seek counseling, or when I think I have a past wound to process, or when I am least expecting it!

But they talk about a relationship with God where you sense His thoughts all the time, and feel Him present constantly. They call it "Immanuel (God with Us) Lifestyle," or, "the interactive presence of God," meaning a continual sense of God being with me where I can sense His heart at any given moment of time. Dr. Karl Lehman has dedicated his life's work to seeking to understand how our physical brain helps us sense God or hinders us from sensing Him. It seems that the key piece we have been missing is this interactive appreciation piece.

Dr. Wilder and Dr. Lehman teach that appreciation is the most important aspect to sensing God's presence. Using brain science to back it up, as well as Scripture, they have taught us to practice remembering times when we have felt thankful or appreciative, as well as times when we have sensed God in the past. Intentionally remembering my physical sensations, as well as my emotions, helps my entire heart, soul, mind, and body connect with God. No wonder Paul tells us in 1 Thessalonians 5:19 to be thankful in everything. I don't think he meant to be thankful *for* everything, but *in* everything.

If, no matter what is happening to me, I can bring to mind an interactive memory of being with my Creator, feeling the appreciation flow through my mind, soul, and body, then I will be able to sense my Papa with me in the current situation! It is a brilliant plan. I may not be able to thank God for what is happening, but I can nestle into memories of appreciation and harness their strength to lead me to His presence, so that I can hear His perspective on my present situation!

As a family, we have begun practicing remembering our joy-filled stories, sharing these stories out loud, and asking God how He feels about being with us. This question is indeed radical. Many people find it difficult to ask because it triggers all of their feelings of shame that God would not want to be with them. Leaning into this fear and pressing into the unknown has brought about monumental changes in us. I can already tell the difference in my own prayer life, as well as in the mood of our family.

Now, after just a few months of intentional appreciation practice followed by listening, I sense You guiding me with the kids, with finances, with how to respond to my husband and others. I sense images *regularly* and some have even been prophetic in nature. When I ask if these are really from You, I hear, "Trust what you see."

Something new has begun in me. Somehow I feel like the spiritual world is breaking through into my physical world, and I am feeling centered more and more in between the two.

May 5, 2011 – Angels Protecting

A few days ago, I was so frustrated with life. I felt like we were under severe spiritual attack. My children were sick. I had a strange fever that would not leave. The washing machine broke. The water pipes outside burst. There were conflicts in our community.

Now, lying in bed with a fever, pushed beyond all emotional and physical limits, I decide to go to appreciation and ask God what He thinks about all of this.

I go the throne of Jesus, the one He carried me to that day I was crying. I am there sitting on the ground with my head in His lap. His gentle hand brushes my hair out of my face. I immediately feel safe and cared for. My body relaxes and fear is driven away.

"What do I need to know about all of the spiritual attack that is coming at us, Jesus?" I ask.

An image comes to me of warrior angels all around our house forming a dome from the ground to the sky. They are on guard, prepared for battle.

Then I sense the words, "I am protecting you, Toni. Only what I can use for your good will get through to you. Trust Me."

Was this God or just me? I still don't know for sure, but I know that the images bring relief to my body, mind, and soul. The tension has left my shoulders. I breathe deep. I can not thank God for all the chaos that our family has been thrown into, but I can thank Him that I can hear His voice in it! I can now trust that the problems I am facing are for a good reason. I trust they will not take me down, and that God will use everything for our good somehow. In an ironic sort of way, I now have a new appreciation memory that has come in the midst of these problems!

May 8, 2011 – Let Me Enjoy You

I am worn. The reality of raising two little babies and a pre-teen in a foreign country is wearing me down. I want to be with God. As I sit and remember times with Him, I am filled with appreciation for how He has been with me in such tender ways. I breathe deeply. Here I am again, coming in need.

"How do you feel about being with me, Papa?" I ask.

I sense warmth. I see open arms. I feel His desire for me.

"Life is hard right now." I let Him know as if He does not already know everything. "What do I need to know to get through?" This question is still relatively new for me to ask. But it feels so right to have a two-way relationship with Him. I quiet and listen.

The words come softly into my mind: "Come to Me more often, My child. You need to feel My joy and pleasure in you, so you can give it to your children."

"So, it is letting You enjoy me that will give me what I need?" I ask in disbelief. It sounds so basic, so freeing. Come, and let Him enjoy *me*. Okay.

As I try to let Him in, I sense emotions that I need to share. "I am angry, my Lord, tired of the weaknesses I see in others."

"Have compassion for the weaknesses of others, My child. Have compassion."

"I am also scared of overextending myself. I am so sad that we don't have grandparents here for our children. I miss my mom and dad. It is not fair. God, how can You call us to be here without parents and grandparents for us and our kids?"

"I know it is hard. Trust me."

I am sad still, but I feel hope. Somehow I feel parented by Him. Is this possible? He wants to parent me? Is this what the Bible means when it says we must become like little children to enter the Kingdom of God? I smile as I think of it. "Yes, my Lord, I will come more often. I will let You enjoy me."

CHAPTER 11

For Personal Reflection and Practice

As you can see, it took many months and many hours of quieting, practicing interactive appreciation, and letting God enjoy me in order for me to begin to feel safe, held, seen, and guided on a regular basis. This work is not something you can do for one year of your life and be done with. It is much like physical exercise, we have to constantly turn our minds to moments where we are fully present, fully alive, and aware of the amazing gift each breath is, each relationships is, each moment is. Our brain is pretty much a muscle after all, so why would it function any differently than our other muscles?

This reality brings to mind Philippians 4:8 where Paul said, "Finally, beloved, whatever is true, whatever is honorable, whatever is just, whatever is pure, whatever is lovely, whatever is commendable, if there is any excellence, if there is anything worthy of praise, think about these things."

1. Quiet yourself. Breathe deeply. Think about how your body is feeling. Are you hot or cold? Comfortable? Hurting anywhere? Carrying stress in your shoulders, neck, or back?

2. Think of three moments in nature where you were in awe and felt full of appreciation. List them, and write down how you felt emotionally and how you responded physically.

3. Think of three moments with people where you were full of thankfulness and appreciation. List them, and write down how you felt emotionally and how you responded physically.

4. Think of three moments with God (if you have sensed His presence) where you felt grateful for His presence. List them, and write down how you felt emotionally and how you responded physically.

5. Share these stories throughout the week with two or three other people.

God with *Us*: Confirmation that I am Not Crazy

May 16, 2011 – Rain on San Geronimo

Matt went out to San Geronimo, our retreat center, today to work. Sometime mid-morning, I was drawn to leave my busy schedule and pray. I sat letting my Creator enjoy me and felt drawn to pray for Matt and San Geronimo.

As I began to pray and listen, a story started to unfold in my imagination. Matt was there at the retreat house in the dining room leading a Bible study with the two staff members, elderly women who have practically grown old caring for this place.

I could see through the many windows that it was raining outside. I wondered about the rain, and I sensed God saying that it was His provision. We are still $100,000 short in paying off the purchase of the property. And a payment is coming due soon. But I sensed in the rain the Divine saying, "I have already provided the money. Everything that is needed for this whole project to become a reality, I have provided. It is already on the way. Just like the rain it will come, the financial provision, the spiritual provision, and the emotional provision."

I treasured these images in my heart and went into my day with peace and joy.

Matt got home a few hours later. During lunch together, I could see that he was emotionally distraught.

"How was your morning out at San G?" I asked, curious about his time there.

"Not so great," he replied. "I cried a lot and cried out to God for help... Big time."

He continued to tell me how he went out to San Geronimo to pay the last of our operating funds to a local guy that helps out with the property.

"A pang went through my heart when I signed the paystub," he shared, "because I had to tell our friend that he could not work anymore until there was more funding."

Matt proceeded to tell me the events that followed. "I loaded up the broken lawn tractor in the back of my station wagon (picture half a lawn tractor hanging out the back, going down the highway), and I wept my fear and trepidation all the way to the next town where the shop was. I managed to stop crying long enough to drop off the tractor for repairs. Then I wept and cried out my fear out all the way home, variously yelling and whispering, 'Help, Papa! Help, Papa!' That was my morning." He ended in hopeless despair.

"What time was that?" I asked, wondering if maybe it was the same time I sensed God prompting me to pray for Matt, or my own soul somehow sensing his distress.

"About 10:45," he said, clueless to what I was about to share.

I was amazed. It had been 10:30 exactly when I had felt drawn to leave the day's work and go intercede for my beloved.

As I shared how I had been led to pray for him, and the images that ensued, I could see both confusion and comfort come across Matt's face.

"I can't believe He would prepare you to receive me today, I was so ashamed of my disbelief and fear that I almost didn't want to share with you. And yet, my God had mercy on me and is meeting me where I am and wanting to provide for me? I don't know why I am not hearing Him right now, but I am so glad that He is speaking to me through you, at least."

I am amazed. I am overwhelmed with the importance of following my heart when I sense that I need to pray for someone. I feel like I am a part of something so much bigger than myself. I am humbled and awed and thankful. And, I am expectant.

May 17, 2011 – The First Time

Today, Matt and I came together to listen to You, Papa, regarding what to do financially. We have been underfunded for years now. Every year, You manage to pull us through, but this year we do not see Your hand providing. It is scary.

We started by sharing memories of times when You have spoken to us, provided for us, been with us. And then something amazing happened. We began hearing You together for the first time, sensing Your words to both of us in our time of need.

"Your financial problems are NOT your fault," I say out loud as the words form in my mind. "You are not being punished for 'living above your means.' This is not your fault and there is NO shame. It can happen to anyone, and is, in fact, happening to a lot of people right now."

I start to cry as the image of the rain on San Geronimo comes back into my mind from last week. "I don't know if this is me, or if this is from God, but I just get the sense very clearly of the word, 'Wait,'" I share with Matt. "Wait. The rain is already falling."

I get the sense that God has put a plan in motion to rescue us. We just do not yet see it. These impressions scare me a little because I do not know if I am making this up, or if this is really from God. My spiritual eyes seem dull still. But with the images and the very real physical things happening around us these days, it is almost as if the spiritual world and the physical world are converging before our eyes.

As tears fall down both of our faces, the words continue to come to Matt: "This financial crisis doesn't scare *Me!*" he senses Jesus say. "Love each other well through this. Wait, and believe what I have told you."

I knew we were in a Holy moment, a moment that would go down in our history as a couple. In our 20 years of praying together, this was the first time we have actually heard God speaking to us, to both of us. And He used each of us to encourage the other. We ended our time feeling peaceful and purposeful. We are to wait, to trust, and to love each other well, and somehow the rest will be taken care of.

May 19, 2011 – Provided For

Today, I was teaching a seminar and received a message from Matt during my break that we had just received a $1300 gift from a Sunday school class who had been moved months earlier to have a garage sale for us! Then, he found out that someone else pledged another $3000 for San Geronimo! God was already working to provide two days ago when we met to pray. With reason, He told us to wait! We did indeed hear His voice!

In Matt's words, Papa had said to us, "Wait. Don't panic. Don't make a knee jerk reaction. Trust that you have heard Me up to this point. Trust that I am compassionate, loving, providing. Trust that I don't miss a trick. Trust that this situation does not scare Me. I have handled bigger."

My heart is overflowing with the fullness of thanksgiving and joy! I am indeed a part of something much bigger than myself! It is so dark and scary to not be in control and to not know where we are going. But it is extremely comforting to know that we are not crazy, that there really is a Divine Being who loves us, cares for us, and is walking with us through this darkness in such a gentle way that we do not have to fear. We just have to look to Him, and that seems to be getting easier the more He enters into our physical reality.

I wonder what He will do next.

May 2011 – Experimental Communal "Listening"

There we were last night – Greg, Alexia, Matt, and I – risking it all to try and sense God's presence with us. We had never tried to listen like this together before, so it seemed a little scary and awkward. As we all took turns sharing our appreciation moments, I could already sense Jesus there.

Then we asked Him, "How do You feel about being with us?"

I could see Him sitting in front of us, just enjoying us. He seemed excited to be with us, like He was excited that we were seeking Him out to be with Him together and to listen. Seeing a smile on His face, I heard Him begin, "I knew you all before you were even born. I called out to each one of you. I stopped the generational forces of evil in each of your lives that sought to take you. And even back then, I had this day in mind." He seemed so satisfied.

I just enjoyed Him enjoying us for a while, His eyes tender, sweet. I shared with the others what I was sensing, not knowing what was going on in their minds.

Then I sensed Him speaking to me, "Toni, you are doing exactly what you need to be doing during this season of life: fighting to remain in Me, to rest, to be aware of My presence in the midst of your crisis. That is exactly what you should be doing and you're doing well. Keep it up."

My mind struggled to hold on to all of this. "Jesus, You seem so carefree, so loving, but isn't there more to You than this?" I said out loud. I know He is the God of the universe, Creator of everything, and yet He always meets me gently where I am.

His gaze became very serious. Then it was as if heaven opened up and power flowed down between Him and God.

Holding my gaze in the stream of light, He responded, "You have no idea the power I wield... you can only handle this much of Me for now. You do not know My power..." I shared with the group what I was sensing.

And after a brief pause, He added, "But I want you to."

Matt sensed that we were to put all of our problems into our own individual bags and set them at the feet of Jesus. We took some time and did just that.

Then Alexia shared, "Toni, you are not going to believe what was happening in my mind as you were sharing what you were seeing and hearing. I was asking Jesus questions, and He was answering them through you. Everything He spoke to you was a direct answer to me!"

How can it be? I do not know, but I want to know more of the power of my God.

Today, I came across Exodus 9:16: "But for this purpose I have raised you up, to show you my power, so that my name may be proclaimed in all the earth."

Make us strong enough to see Your power, Oh God, and may Your name be proclaimed in all the earth through us, Your people!

CHAPTER 12

For Personal Reflection and Practice

1. Quiet yourself. Then go to one of your appreciation moments. Ask God how He feels about being with you.

2. Ask yourself and God if there is anyone you feel led to pray for. If a person comes to mind, hold them in your thoughts and ask Jesus if there is anything He wants you to know regarding that person. Write down everything you sense.

3. Would you ever be willing to "listen" to God with someone else? If not, what are your reservations? Share those with Jesus and ask Him what He thinks about that.

4. Do you know anyone who would be crazy enough to "listen" to God with you? Ask God if there is someone in your life who He has prepared for you to enter into a deeper spiritual plane with.

CHAPTER 13

He is the Strong One

May 25, 2011 – I Stand Corrected

For two years now Matt and I have been trying on new roles in our marriage. For 20 years, Matt was the more melancholic of the two of us, and I was the upbeat one who seemed to be able to pull it all together. Unfortunately, that meant that he tended to be unstable, and I tended to be over controlling and contemptuous.

So a few years back, we both found these roles to be unhealthy and decided to ditch them for some healthier, more liberating ones. We decided to give ourselves the freedom and right to be both weak and strong. It has been a journey of self-discovery, and along the way, we have seen glimpses of God.

Last night, I realized Matt was tanking emotionally. I get scared when this happens because when things get tough, sometimes he becomes volatile or he shuts down emotionally, leaving me all alone. Thankfully, we have such a beautiful relationship where we can talk about anything, even these tendencies and my fear.

As I was sharing my concerns with him, I heard myself get

louder and louder. I could feel my pulse quicken and my body prepare for the worst. Then, in a desperate plea, I heard myself cry out, "I don't want to be the strong one anymore."

What happened at that point surprised me tremendously! Immediately, I heard God guffaw and gently rebuke me by stating, "You are NOT the strong one, My darling. I am."

I was jolted out of my self-pity and my fear. I stood refreshingly corrected. Images flashed in my mind of the rain over San Geronimo and the hand that held me when I went into labor with Matty, the peace that came from Him, not from me. I was not strong in those moments, HE was.

Yes, I gladly stood corrected and I smiled. As I laughed out loud, Matt was incredibly curious as to what was happening in my mind and heart.

I apologized and thanked him for being able and willing to listen to me. I told him of our Father's truth breaking through my fearful perspective. I could smile and rest even in this storm because He would be my strength. He would be our strength. Matt was relieved, and our discussion ended with us holding each other and letting Papa God comfort us together.

I nestled down into Papa's protection that night and felt His shield around me. My heart filled with thankfulness that I do not have to be the strong one, and neither does my husband! We can both be weak at the same time, because He is more than capable of being strong for the both of us.

May 2011 – Triangle of Protection

I come today to sit with God. The pressures of our financial need are present with me, as is my precious husband who is falling apart over it all. He seems angry and unable to trust God. I cannot be strong for both of us. I am reminded to let my Savior be my strength. I do not have to carry us all.

As I kneel in silence, I close my eyes, and I can see myself on my knees praying in my imagination. I glance up and notice three figures standing over me, their arms connected, forming a triangle of protection all around me. Nothing can get to me. I am vulnerable and weak, but not exposed. They are there protecting me. They are Father, Son, and Holy Spirit. I open my eyes and can almost see them in the physical world. I bend back down in my kneeling state and rest. I feel honored, precious, and undone.

Tears flow as I let the weakness come forth and let myself receive His protection.

September 2011 – Breathe

I am so stressed and tired today. The work never seems to end. Physically and emotionally I am empty. I have not had regular time to just sit with my Creator in so long.

I wish I could sleep right now, but there is no time. I will have to pick up one of the kids in just 15 minutes. I might have enough energy to go and quiet and listen, even if the time is brief. I put the work aside and go to the patio where the sun is shining and the birds are singing. I sit down in the garden and settle into an old memory of when God had been there with me in the past. As I remember how my body felt full and light, the thankfulness sweeps over me, and I realize how tired I really am. Tears come as I hear myself saying out loud, "I am so tired. I am so tired. I am so tired," over and over again.

Almost instantly, I sense Him near. Yes, Him… Jesus, or some invention of my mind that seems like Him. In my imagination, He comes to me. He kneels down in front of me. I open my eyes in the present, and I swear, I can see Him there. Is this just my imagination? Or can I really see my Lord right here with me? I don't know. But it feels so amazing.

Surprised by this almost physical appearance, I ask Him, "What do you want, my Lord?" I imagine He has some mission for me, someone to help, something to do. It has to be important for Him to make an appearance like this.

His response catches me off guard, "I want to meet your needs today, My child."

Whoa… That made me uncomfortable, to say the least. I fight back tears and emotionally take a step back. "You are God. I am supposed to come to worship You, not just get from You." I feel vulnerable and scared. I know, I know… I really should know better by now. I mean, that is what happened to the disciples when Jesus knelt down to wash their feet, right? Reading that story and actually experiencing it are two different things for my brain!

"What do you need?" He continues on without missing a beat. My tears find their way out of the darkness, and I begin to sift my soul for what I need most.

Between sobs, I get out four words: rest, remember, re-creation, relationships. It's almost as if He was telling me what I needed. Yes, they all begin with R. I laugh thinking, "What a great sermon that would make," as if that doesn't show how hard it is for me to receive just for me!

With that, I sense Him take my face in His hands, lean toward me, put His face close to mine, almost touching my mouth with His, and say, "Breathe, right now."

I feel nervous, like butterflies are in my stomach. I have been in relationship with Jesus for over 30 years, but it has rarely felt this raw, this intimate. I take a slow, deep breath. And as I inhale, He begins exhaling into my mouth… exhaling rest into my physical body. My lungs expand, and rest begins to flow from there to every part of me. As oxygen flows in my blood, so does His rest.

I am amazed at what He is doing. But at the same time, I feel a little stupid. "What if someone saw me right now, sitting here with my mouth wide open?" I think. "They would think I were crazy!"

As if reading my mind, He responds, "Just stay right here and breathe. Don't worry about what others think."

So I do. I sit in His presence for ten minutes maybe, I am not sure how long. This is so sweet, I don't want it to end. The world has completely stopped for a moment, and I am still. I am receiving, not just emotionally or spiritually, but physically as well.

When I finally open my eyes, I feel revived and sense Him say, "Now, remember. Remember to breathe *Me* every time you are at your end. Just stop and picture Me there in front of you, facing you, and breathe. Now, go play and enjoy your relationships. You do need them."

It is amazing to me that brain science has now proven the extremely healthy effects just sitting and breathing can have on our mind and body. Some call it meditation, others awareness exercises. Jesus knew what I needed today, and He led me there and met me there. I needed to breathe, not just meditative breaths, but the very breath of Life itself. Meditation will never be the same.

October 2011 – Sleep

I come to You so tired, but hungry for You. I feel so empty. Part of me thinks that if I can just read Your Word more, I would feel better. Or maybe if I pray more, I would feel better. But I am so physically tired I keep falling asleep every time I try. What do I need to know, Jesus?

I sense You near. I can see You here with me. You have such compassion on Your face. When will I have that kind of compassion on myself?

"Let Me be your strength," You say as You pick me up and carry me to the bed. You tuck me in, and as You brush my hair from my face You add, "Sleep, My child. You need to sleep. You give so much all of the time. You need to rest."

Thank You for teaching me what I need and when. Thank You for guiltless sleep. Thank You that I can trust that You are working even when I am sleeping.

CHAPTER 13

For Personal Reflection and Practice

1. Do you tend to be the strong one or the weak one in your relationships? Quiet yourself and ask God what He thinks about that dynamic. Journal your impressions.

2. Do you feel safe enough to let yourself be weak? Can you rest when you are tired? Or do you normally push yourself past your limits? I was an athlete all of my life and I was trained to push myself beyond my limits. While in many ways this is a great skill to have, it turns in on me when it is not balanced with resting and learning to receive.

3. How does Jesus treat those who are weak and tired? What verses come to mind?

4. Where do you go to receive? Most of us, especially if we are parents of little ones or work with small children, give all day long. What do you do when you are empty? Ask God if there is anything you need to know about receiving.

5. Share with someone else how you perceive yourself and ask him or her how he or she sees you. Share together ideas of how you can receive on a regular basis so as not to get dangerously tired.

Becoming Free to Be Fully Me

April 28, 2012 – Do Not Compare

Today, Matt and I come to You in prayer. I quiet myself, look for You, and ask how You feel about being with me. I picture You standing there in front of me, and I am bringing to You sand art that I have made. Like a child proud of a scribbled drawing they have worked on with all of their might, I proudly present my work to my Creator. I feel satisfied with what I've done. I know I did good work.

Then, as I present this to You, I look around and see others bringing their work, too. Their creations seem so much more elaborate than mine: glass houses, log cabins, brick bridges. A sinking feeling hits my stomach as my mind begins to compare what I have done with what I see all around me.

"My pitiful contribution doesn't compare with the beauty of other people's work," I confess out loud. "There must be something wrong with me that I can't produce elaborate creations like everyone else," I say, hanging my head in shame.

"My child," Jesus interrupts, "don't compare yourself with

others. Before you saw anyone else's work, what did *you* think about yours? How do you feel about what you've done?"

Thinking back to just a few seconds ago, my countenance brightens and I respond, "I was very pleased with what I have done. I was as eager as a little child to show my Papa what I had worked so hard on. I was satisfied that I had given it my best."

Still not completely convinced that what I have done is good enough, I look to Him and ask, "What do *You* think about my work? Why is theirs so much better than mine?"

Jesus looks compassionately down at me, caresses my face with His hand, and says, "Not all are given the same materials to work with, Toni. I gave them wood, glass, and brick. I gave you sand. Have you been faithful with the sand you have been given?"

"Yes, Papa, I have been as faithful as I can possibly be with the sand that You have given me," I reply, knowing that I gave myself completely to my creation.

I look down at my work again and then back at the work of the others. A twinge of grief pierces my chest as wonder why I was only given sand.

"That is not for you to know, My child," Jesus replies with a soothing smile. "Just keep your eyes on Me and pay attention to your own story. How well *others* do with what I've given them is none of your business."

Even though He is correcting me, He does it in such a validating, compassionate way. I feel freed to enjoy my own work again. Some might want to make fun of what I produce, but my God knows the effort I put into my work. It is only His opinion that matters. This is my story, and I am the only one responsible for how it is lived.

It's still hard to not look around and wish I were someone else, or wish that I could be as productive as the others I see. But each time I am tempted, I will picture my sand art in my head and remember that Jesus doesn't want me to be someone else. He wants me to be fully me.

May 16, 2012 – Let Me be Your Father

This week, I have struggled to let myself rest, play a game, veg-out, or even sleep. I feel selfish for not "producing" something. I have to do a lot of self-talk to stay out of shame land.

I was sick yesterday, and all day long, I fought voices in my head saying, "You're lazy. You will never amount to anything." Papa, where does this come from? Is it just my inner parent? If so, why is she so hard on me still? And if not, could this be spiritual attack?

Some memories surface, times when my coaches pushed me too far in sports. I was never allowed to rest or get tired. Then the memory of that time I broke my leg comes to mind. I remember how my dad, not realizing it was broken, told me to walk on it anyway.

I am sad for the little girl in me that was never allowed to rest. I am just now coming to know my true heart more and more. That helps tremendously. But, Father, who am I in Your eyes?

Words come into my mind, and I sense His presence, "My child, you are a hard worker when motivated by a relational cause. You like a good challenge, but after you've activated something, you're ready to move on. You are faithful to your friends. You are generous with your time and your possessions. You are very active and love sports, crafts, and karaoke. You do the hard things first and then rest and play later. You are constantly producing, and you feel alive when you are giving your all to whatever you are engaged in.

"You must learn that when you are not this person, it is because you need to get away and rest. It is not like you to be unmotivated, depressed, or lagging behind."

"Come to me all who labor..." (Matthew 11:28).

It never occurred to me that if I was not "producing," it was because I needed to rest! I just heard "lazy" in my mind. This will take some practice in noticing. I want Your yoke, Papa. Mine is too heavy. I cannot be the superwoman I feel driven to be. I want to be the beloved child.

My Creator responds, "I want to be your Father. I want to meet the needs your earthly father did not meet and is not meeting for you. Yes, he is a wonderful dad, and he does his very best to love you. However, his best is not enough for what you need. No father's love is, except Mine. Look to Me for recognition. Look to Me when you want to be 'seen.'"

"Oh, Father, thank You for wanting me as Your own. I want to be Your baby girl!"

June 7, 2012 – I am Training You

Father, we are in so much debt right now with San Geronimo, with ourselves. Please provide what we need. I do not understand what You are doing. Have we missed the mark? I feel like I am at the Red Sea with my family and my community. We are waiting for You to part it, or send us jet skis or something so that we can go over it. Yet You delay. One by one, the soldiers begin to attack, and we scramble to fight them off, all the while waiting, trusting that You will save us. Will You? Or did we miss Your will – Your direction?

John the Baptist comes to my mind. You let him die in prison when You were just across the city. You could have saved him, but You chose not to. Will You let us be put to shame? We have trusted You when so few have. Show Yourself the mighty God You are. Do not let us be put to shame! You are our only hope!

"Toni, as I said to John the Baptist, I say to you: blessed is he who does not stumble because he does not understand what I am doing (Matthew 11:6, paraphrase). As you wait for Me to come through for San Geronimo, you are training others."

I can hear Him getting excited at this point. "You are modeling for others how to get back to joy, how to be with Me even in hopeless despair. I am also giving you opportunities to practice coming to Me. I am growing your capacity to endure emotionally difficult realities. A good leader is one who can stay themselves and remain in My presence even in the most traumatic situation."

I am smiling by now. He has not abandoned. He is not just playing games with us. He is training us! I breathe a sigh of deep relief, confident that I truly can trust Him.

"The Thrive training is from me," He continues. "It is the pearl of great price, for this training is bringing you to receive from Me in ways you can only begin to imagine. This is what matters in life. This is all that matters in life, being able to sense Me with you in every situation, no matter how difficult. I know your heart, Toni. This is what you want for every soul on the planet. I will use you to help others remove what hinders them from sensing Me close to them."

"Oh, Papa! You do know my heart. I would be honored to help others sense You with them. I gladly give my life to follow You into this dream."

Matthew 10:27 comes to mind. I look it up and am again in awe of my God. "What I tell you in the dark, say in the light, and what you hear whispered, proclaim on the housetops."

I will follow You, Papa. Lead on.

August 16, 2012 – Snuggled Close

"I come to You today so thankful that I have time to be alone with You. How do You feel about being with me?" I jump right in. Babies are napping and time is short.

I see You put me on Your lap and squeeze me and snuggle me close. I feel peace, warmth, rest. I think of my little babies and how the very first thing I want to do with them in the morning is cuddle them. It is also the first thing they seek when they wake up. They want to be held. And then, throughout the day, they are constantly watching me, observing, learning, and doing what I do. I find it so precious.

May I be that way with You, Papa. Curled up in Your arms, attentive to Your every action. Where will You go? What will You say? I am here.

CHAPTER 14

For Personal Reflection and Practice

1. My "inner parent" tends to be critical and say things like, "You are lazy. You will never accomplish anything great!" Do you have inner voices like that? Write down any critical voices you may hear sometimes. Ask God where these voices come from. Usually this "parent voice" wants to help us succeed, but, unfortunately, at some point in life, it was trained to use manipulation and shame to control us instead of love and grace. Ask God what you need to know about this in your life.

2. Who are you really? What is your true heart like? Maybe your parents have told you all of your life the ways in which you are uniquely you. But, maybe they did not, and you do not really know the characteristics of your true heart. Spend time this week asking those who enjoy you the most what unique characteristics they see in you. Also, spend time asking God what He sees in you that is uniquely you. Write these traits down so that you know who it is like you to be when you are rested and at your best.

3. In what ways does Papa God want to Father or Mother you? Ask yourself and God what kind of parenting you need most in your life right now.

4. While part of a parent's role is to enjoy their children, another role is to give their children the bigger perspective that they do not yet see, especially in difficult or adverse circumstances. Is there a situation right now that you do not understand? Perhaps an unsolvable problem? Quiet yourself, go to appreciation, and ask Jesus what you need

to know about this situation. How does it end? Remember to pay attention to images, impressions, sensations, feelings or thoughts that surface.

CHAPTER 15

Let the Training Begin

July 13, 2012 – Live in Me

We are currently at Thrive, the relational skills-based, leadership training program with the Life Model Works organization. We have prepared an entire year and a half in order to attend Track I of the training. It is like nothing I have ever done before. It is all skills-based exercises we do with our bonded partner. All of the exercises are designed to increase our ability to feel joy, quiet, and shalom, that feeling you get when everything is in the right place, at the right time, in the right amount.

One of the exercises we are doing asks us to look for memories of interacting with God that reflect His different aspects as Father, Son, and Holy Spirit.

The memory I most relate to God the Father is the one where I was in His hand on the way to the hospital to have Matty. I felt held, completely safe, and at peace.

Another one comes to mind when I felt like I was in the womb and the darkness was as light to Him.

For Jesus, the Son, I have the memory of celebrating the King, when He saw me in my distress and carried me back to His throne. I also see the memory of the Shepherd in my mind, holding His little lamb, and then, enjoying her as she turned into a little baby.

When I think of the Holy Spirit, I remember the time on the beach when sparkles appeared everywhere. It felt like the Holy Spirit was dancing all around me, celebrating me, drawing me into awe and wonder.

Holy Creator, what do You want me to know about each aspect of Your character? I sense He is so elated to be spending this time with me, playing in my imagination, nurturing my soul.

"As Father, I am protecting you. I am powerful, and yet, I hold you in My hands. You are safe. You are not alone. Remember, even the darkness is as light to Me.

"As Jesus, the Son, I 'see' you, and I see all of your needs. I am tender towards you, and I enjoy you immensely.

"As the Holy Spirit, I think you are so special. I celebrate you. I want to enter into you, to dwell with you, in your entire body, mind, and soul, comforting you, and giving you peace and courage."

I sense them come around me, overlay their arms, and form a cone of protection that is completely impenetrable, like the one I had seen on my knees in prayer not long ago.

I feel positively overwhelmed. It is too much joy for me to take in. I feel like nothing can hurt me. There is nothing else in the world that matters more than being right here with my Maker. It is almost like, deep within my body, soul, and mind, I am experiencing that God can get me through anything.

"What do You ask of me, Creator?" I can think of no other way to respond but to offer my life. "Here I am, send me."

"I just want you to enjoy and rest for now, My love. The time for action will come. Practice living in Me in this new way for now."

I am surprised. I have been trained all of my life that I am blessed to be a blessing. And I know that is true. However, it amazes me that God Himself would pause between the two and validate that it is enough for now that I just enjoy Him and rest. I have time to play and practice sensing Him. I actually get to be blessed, first! I feel relieved and cherished. Thank You.

June 18, 2012 – I Made You

I am sitting with God in prayer, coming to listen to Him for whatever He wants to talk to me about. As I quiet, my imagination sees us in the garden where we sometimes go to talk. He is older in this image, much like a Father. He takes my hand and we begin to dance cheek to cheek.

"What would You like to do in me today?" I ask.

My mind suddenly sees me in the second grade. I am sitting in my desk on the front row frantically working to finish my assignments before anyone else in the class. I smile as I remember that year. I can see myself looking at the chalkboard, writing down the assignments, and then quickly glancing over my shoulder at the person behind me to make sure they were not ahead of me. I have to say, it kind of annoyed the person behind me. I can remember them covering their work and telling me to stop!

"Why was I like this, Papa? Was this a good thing or bad thing?" I wonder.

"Well," He answers with a question, "how do you feel in this memory?"

I begin to reflect. "I'm energized. My adrenaline is flowing. It's a rush to keep ahead of everyone else. It was fun for me, almost like a game. But it did tend to bother everyone else, even the teacher. I remember her getting on me regularly for starting the work too early! In reality, I think I was bored stiff. The work seemed so easy that I just wanted to get it done. I also notice that I wanted to shine. I wanted to be the best."

"I made you that way," Jesus responds, smiling at me, almost laughing.

"Why?" I ask Him, feeling like this competitiveness was a

curse instead of a gift. "I was so immature, and I obviously annoyed others by my competitive nature."

"I made you, not to shine at the expense of others, but to inspire others to be their best. I made you to not settle for mediocrity! I want you to burn brightly for others to see Me in you. I did not make you this way so that others will look bad or feel jealous, but that they might be encouraged. That is why you became a cheerleader, is it not? You have always cheered others on and wanted them to be their best, too. For you, it was not only about you being the best. You want everyone to be their best! I love that about you! I made you that way."

This feels so embarrassing, so vulnerable.

"Now that you have given up your defense mechanism of pride and are learning to walk with Me, you will be free to shine in ways that do not hurt others, but inspire them to greatness, My child," He finishes with an excited, satisfied look on His face. It is extremely exposing to think of how intimately He knows me and has been patiently walking with me to bring me to this point. He never grows impatient with me.

"All this time, I have been afraid to shine," I explain to Him. "It seems like when I did shine, other people felt bad, felt less than. So I would try to hide, even hide my relationship with You, Papa, for fear that others would feel bad if they didn't hear You the way I did. But You're telling me that it is okay to shine, to follow You in giving my best to the world, not so that I am seen as great, but so that others can see YOU?"

Your perspective is like a cool breeze on a warm day. I feel relieved, beautiful, and freed to be all You have created me to be.

August 2012 – Enjoy the Ride

I have spent the last month remembering and enjoying all of the "Immanuel moments" I encountered during our Thrive training. We are back in Uruguay now, and all I can think is how safe I felt in the States. Here I feel spiritually exposed and in danger most of the time. It is almost like a mother wildebeest with her calves trailing behind the herd out in the open, vulnerable to the cheetahs. Under the stress of living in Uruguay, I start to mentally break down, lose perspective, dis-integrate, and question my identity non-stop.

I remember what a friend shared with me when we were at our training. He came up to me after I told a story of when I had sensed Your presence. He put his hand on my shoulder and said, "While you were telling your story, I saw two angels guarding over you. One was on each side of your body protecting you. When I asked God what I should know about it, he said they were fire angels, and they would burn everything that was attacking you and purify it for God's use."

As I remember this moment, the words nurture my exposed soul. The truth is that I am not exposed. You are protecting me.

I go from there to the garden where I sometimes find You as Papa, God. You appear and we begin to walk and talk, but I notice we are not alone. This time, I sense a host of angels all around me, an army, like they are on their way somewhere to do battle.

"Papa? What about San Geronimo?" I continue to ask, wondering if He will give me some kind of assurance.

"I have provided for San Geronimo," He says with a peaceful smile, tapping my hand that's tucked into His arm as we walk.

"Is there anything I need to do?" I know that if I could just DO something, I would feel more in control.

"Believe the image of rain that I gave you," He wistfully says, His face playful, light, and fun. I brace myself for what is to come.

He takes me by the hand and begins swinging me in circles until He lifts me off the ground and adds, "And enjoy the ride!"

This is a great adventure to Him. He sees a reality in which I can sit back and enjoy all of the ups and downs and out of control feelings that following Him brings. Almost like a roller coaster. We can enjoy it because we trust the tracks are strong and are leading us to the right place.

The crazy thing is that in real life, when you can't see the tracks, enjoying a risk-filled adventure can seem impossible to do, even illogical. To be in financial crisis and yet be in a wild emotional space enjoying the story as it unfolds – knowing there is a happy ending. It defies the laws of gravity.

Please help me to do just that, Papa. Help me model for my husband and my children a radical faith that can enjoy the unpredictable ride of trusting You, even when we don't see the tracks.

Deuteronomy 9:3 comes to mind: "Be assured today that the Lord your God is the one that goes across ahead of you like a devouring fire. He will destroy them; He will subdue them before you."

August 18, 2012 – Look at Me

I come to You, Jesus, absolutely distraught. I just finished meeting with a precious young woman. She shared with me her very painful story of growing up in an abusive home. I introduced her to You and watched her receive Your love for the first time in her life. It was beautiful how she could sense Your presence with her. But she still lives with her abusers, and I know I will never get to see her again.

I am broken over her life situation. It's like I can feel her pain. What do I need to know about this? As I look at You, I begin to sob. The pain wells up from deep within like a tidal wave washing over me, and I look away in anger.

"It's not fair! It's not fair that children have to suffer so grotesquely, that their parents can scream, fight, abuse them, and they just have to suffer it. I feel their pain, Papa. And I don't know what to do with it!"

In my mind, I am transported to a desert wasteland. There are two chairs facing each other. I am in one, Jesus in the other. We are almost close enough that our knees can touch. All around us is war, starvation, natural disasters, crime, and pain.

"Look at Me, Toni."

"I can't."

"Look at Me," He says firmly, yet gently, as He takes my face in His hands and turns me so that my eyes meet His.

As I look at Him, I can tell He feels my pain, but I notice that there is more than just pain there. He knows something, something I don't know. My mind goes back to the girl.

I look away. "She needs community, Papa. She has no one, and yet Matt and I cannot be there for her. I introduced her to You, but will You be enough for her?" I can hardly believe I've said this.

Jesus turns my face to His again and speaks very measuredly, "You have to learn that I am enough. I do not need you. You will have to learn this, or I cannot use you to do what I have planned for you. Do not fight it. Stay with Me and trust Me with others.

"And regarding all the pain that is around us," He says, addressing the imagery in my mind, "I know a bigger story. I know how all of this ends. I know you do not understand how I can endure all of the suffering that happens all over the world every day. But you have to trust Me. Instead of looking around at all of the suffering, keep looking into My eyes. Keep my eyes so close to you that they are bigger than any problems around you."

It is the way He looks deep into my soul as He speaks His truth that transforms me. Anyone else could say these same words, but they would fall on deaf ears. He speaks them from within my own soul.

I feel calmed. Held. I can trust Him. In my imagination, I picture this young woman in my hands and hand her over to our Creator. "Please take her, Papa."

He gladly takes her, draws her into His arms, and holds her. That is where I will leave her, and I know she will be safe with Him.

CHAPTER 15

For Personal Reflection and Practice

1. Look for memories of interacting with God that reflect His different aspects as Father, Son, and Holy Spirit. Write down at least one memory from each category if you can. Remember to notice your physical sensations and your emotions in each memory.

2. While reflecting on these interactive memories, ask God what He wants you to know about each aspect of His character. What does this have to do with you?

3. Spend time receiving from Him.

If you are unable to sense His presence do not worry. Keep practicing appreciation. Also, practice enjoying those around you and letting them enjoy you. It is all connected, and sometimes we need to feel enjoyed by a human in the flesh before we can sense how much God enjoys us! Strange, I know, but joy and appreciation are essential for our brains to function and sense God the way we were created to do.

PART IV

• • • • •

*Learning to Receive
(2012-2013)*

Golden Moments

September 2014

The world is gray today, but for the glow of golden hair
That bobs up and down and shines with golden flare.
The trees are bending, the applause is clear
The green grass a stage as the babes draw near.

They laugh and dance and roll in the dew
Their eyes on Mommy and Daddy, it's true
They need their audience, their people, their fans
To enjoy them, to smile for them, and clap their hands.

An act so simple, yet so profound
To enjoy our children as they goof around
To stop the world on a gray day
And see the golden moments that can otherwise slip away.

It is a million of these joyful encounters that bind our hearts
They fill our souls and help us when our world falls apart.
Presence is priceless, it has the power to give us resilience
If we can stop, sense, feel, and enjoy those who are with us.

CHAPTER 16

My Needs are Valid

November 28, 2012 – Running Ahead

Today, I was singing karaoke for my time with You, Papa, and I was torn to shreds. The song was Cyndi Lauper's "Time after Time" that speaks of a relationship where one person is running ahead of the other. In the chorus, the one following calls out, asks their lover to slow down, and promises to be there for them when they are lost or when they fall.

I finished the song heaving in tears. I have run ahead, and You are wondering if I'm okay. I slow and fall behind so You can catch me.

"Why do I run ahead?" I wonder. "Is it too painful to stay in the present?"

I crumble at Your feet under so much weight. All of the kids' emotional instability, the demands I feel from pastoring our church community, our financial crisis, my husband's well-being, the physical demands of daily life here... I crumble under it all. I used to be so strong, or at least I thought I was. Oh, Papa, I am so weak – physically and emotionally.

I see Him here in my karaoke room with me, looking at me with compassion.

"This doesn't surprise You, does it?" I say, as I look up into His eyes. I can see so much through the way He looks at me. "You're actually glad I realize this?" I need verification that I am reading Him right.

"My child, it is because you know how weak you are that I can use you. Don't hate your weakness."

"But I do. I despise that I am so fragile! I want to be invincible, physically and emotionally! I want to play tennis again and run with my children. I want to carry all the weight of our life with no problem. I want to *not* have needs." The truth in its most pure form finally comes out into the light.

"Why is that, My precious one?"

"Because if I have needs, then I have to depend on others to meet them. And either they will fail, or if they do come through, I will owe them something." My thinking is darker than I knew.

"No, My child, you won't. You are free to just love others. There is no need to fix, lead, or guide; just love them and enjoy them. I made you to need. Your weakness is not a result of the Fall. Your despising your need is a result of the Fall. It is hard for you to need because when you needed, you were not provided for, or you were taken advantage of."

"Papa, I miss my parents so much. I'm so thankful for them and for all You've done to restore us. I'm thankful that they help me rest and play: karaoke, movies, walks, long baths, cards, sports. They did such a good job never burdening me as a child with their problems. They really did a good job containing their troubles.

"I'm tired of bearing the weight of all of the work. Help me ask for help when I need it, to ask for rest when I need it, and not be ashamed. I realize I am ashamed of having needs, and I am scared to ask for help."

"Embrace that I made you this way, My child. You making space for your own needs to be met is the best way you can teach your children that their needs are valid. Modeling this for your children and others in your community will help create a community that has compassion for weakness."

January 23, 2013 – Need to Rest

Today, I was with some dear friends at San Geronimo having a time of prayer. They had come for spiritual discernment and asked if we would listen with them to what God might want them to know. I had no idea God had something for me as we began to pray!

Preparing my heart to listen for my friends, I asked Jesus how He felt about being with me. I sensed a huge lion standing in front of me. His head was as big as my body, much like Aslan in the Chronicles of Narnia. He was so powerful, yet so tender and soft. I was not afraid, but mesmerized, awed.

Coming close, He began to nuzzle me. I could almost physically feel His mane brushing up against my face! I sensed Him enjoying me to the core of who I am. While there were no words, the images were enough to bring a smile across my face, goose bumps up and down my body, and a small giggle as if someone where tickling me. Thankful for this precious gift, I then began listening for our friends. Our time was beautiful, and while I was incredibly satisfied, I could feel the exhaustion of the week catching up with me.

By the afternoon, I was struggling to hang on. I thought we were going to have the night free to rest with no visitors, but even before our guests from last night could leave, more people were showing up.

I was confused. Matt and I had discussed this already. He knew that we needed a break from people, a time to unwind and care for our young family and ourselves. I felt the anger rise, "Why did he invite them and not tell me? Why does it seem to me that he neglects our needs and ONLY looks out for the needs of others?"

My thoughts raced as feelings whirled inside of me like a tornado: unprotected, unwanted, undesired, abused, and taken advantage of. What do I do with all of this unbridled energy? I knew I did not want to hurt anyone, especially my husband, but this had to be addressed. I could not continue without rest.

I got alone, took deep breaths, and looked for Jesus, "Where are You? What do I need to know?"

He appeared almost as soon as the words left my lips.

"I am here." He was right in front of me in the form of the Lion from earlier today. Hope like sunshine burst through the swirling feelings that were causing havoc in my soul.

As He nuzzled me, my heart rate calmed, and I could hear Him explaining to me what was happening.

"You are maturing, My child. You are sensing that you and Matt need to pay attention to your own needs and care for yourselves better. You are no good if you are empty. It is valid that you feel the way you do. You are angry with Matt for not considering your needs more. I can understand that. But what you don't realize is that YOU need to learn to consider your needs more. Remember you are not a victim. You have options here. This is your chance to grow. Bring your needs to Me, let Me meet them, and then the way forward will be clearer."

Without hesitating, I began to put to words all of the need I felt within. "I need to be desired, to be seen, to be safe, to be protected." The tears fall. "I feel so sad," I add as I let the grief whirl around. I close my eyes and feel Him right in front of me, nuzzling me, enjoying me.

How He began to fill me, I cannot say. It did not involve words, but I could feel strength coming into my weak places, as I lingered in His presence. I felt how He desires me. I sensed how beautiful He thinks I am. He is so happy when I am with Him, even in my tornado of potentially destructive emotions.

A smile came across my face because in the midst of deep pain, I felt His joy. I could feel how proud of me He is, and I could feel His strength calling me to forgive my husband and invite him into a new reality, a new way of thinking and living.

I wanted to forgive because Jesus Himself had met my needs. I was no longer a desperate beggar trying to get others to care for me. No, I was at a banquet table that was so full I could invite others to join me.

I opened my eyes, found Matt, and lovingly asked if we could talk. It was not easy. It was one of our hardest conversations ever, but when it got tough, I just closed my eyes and could see, hear, and feel the Lion of Judah with me, soothing me, guiding me, giving me words.

I let Matt know that I needed to rest, that I could not give that up for anyone right now. I invited him to see our needs as important and valid. Then I asked him to help brainstorm some options of what to do with our unexpected guests.

After much discussion and many tears, Matt decided to own his people pleasing tendencies. He confessed how he couldn't say "no" to the people wanting to come, and how he thought we could just deal with it. He asked me for forgiveness and shared how he wants to value our needs for rest and downtime. Then he decided to make things right by explaining to our friend all that had happened and asking if he could reschedule his trip in a few days.

Our friend more than understood and was willing to give us the much needed time alone. I cannot explain how different I feel on the inside. Usually, I guilt myself into giving more than I can give. I convince myself that others' needs are more important than mine and that I am to serve "sacrificially." Jesus is teaching me that I am worth taking time to be filled. I will be able to serve others when I have let Him serve me!

I am filled with gratitude that my Savior, my Lord, my Creator would care enough about the inner workings of my soul to come, calm the storm inside, and show me the way forward.

April 8, 2013 – Daily Bread

Today, I sensed God showing me all of our moments together thus far: times when He held me, walked with me, breathed His rest into me, carried me for days, looked me in the eyes with joy, called me by name.

I asked, "What do You want me to know regarding all of these memories?"

"DO NOT FORGET! That was the biggest sin of My people in the Old Testament. They forgot the great things I had done for them. Remember every one of these moments. Make this remembering your daily bread instead of the fears that come your way. DO NOT FEAR! Remember and tell the stories. I will be here for you. Do not fear the future."

Then I saw an image of Him standing over me with His hands on my head as if He were guarding my thoughts. The passage from 2 Corinthians 10:5 comes to mind: "We demolish arguments and every pretension that sets itself up against the knowledge of God, and we take captive every thought to make it obedient to Christ" (NIV). It is as if He is there helping me take thoughts captive and defeat the pretensions by remembering what He has done in my life.

I feel warm and relaxed, like the memories are filling up my mind and pushing out all of the fear. I feel a sense of purpose come over me. I am to remember the great things God has done for me and tell the stories.

April 9, 2013 – Missing Matt

Matt is away on an out of town trip for the week. I am missing him, truly missing him. In the past, I would miss his help, I think, more than him. With three children in a foreign country, the daily tasks of living can be so overwhelming sometimes. But this is different. This time, I am missing him, his smile, his hugs, his warmth, and his listening ear.

While this is healthy, I do not like missing him! It hurts. My brain wants to detach from him altogether, so that I don't have to feel the pain of longing for him. Part of me wants to be really angry at him for leaving me alone, but I believe in what he is doing. And I know that he had to be away, he did not want to go. This is so complicated! Attachment pain is such a tricky thing!

Instead of detaching, working, or eating, I decide to go to my Papa God. "Papa, I don't understand why I feel all this pain and loss, and why I feel so alone. He's only going to be gone for a week! Is there anything You want me to know?"

The image from yesterday of Him standing over me guarding my thoughts comes to mind. And words begin to penetrate my soul. "**You are not alone**. Dwell on the stories. Live in them. And know, **there is nowhere else Matt would rather be than in your arms.** That is true! Receive it, Toni. It may feel uncomfortable, but it is true!"

I am caught off guard. He has just revealed something in me that runs very deep, and I do not understand it. For some reason, it is easier for me to feel abandoned and blame Matt for all of my discomfort and pain, than to feel deeply loved and miss him... Why?

Jesus gently answers my thoughts. "You may never know why... But I am here guarding your mind during this time. Just let yourself receive."

This feels so new to me. I want to feel loved and miss Matt, instead of feeling abandoned and angry. I let Jesus' words sink in, and I grab my phone and play my and Matt's "song" from 1990 by the Seventy Seven's, "There is nowhere else I'd rather be than in your arms..." I begin to remember. I see us dancing in our favorite field, playing in the mud. I remember our long talks throughout the night when we felt understood and not alone. I receive. And I let myself feel deeply loved, and I genuinely miss my husband. As a tear sneaks out of my eye, a smile simultaneously takes over my face, and I feel eight years old again, grieving loss, but feeling loved and not alone.

CHAPTER 16

For Personal Reflection and Practice

1. Can you identify your physical and emotional needs and lovingly invite others to help meet those? Or do you expect others to figure out your needs and meet them without you having to ask?

2. Are you able to protect your space for rest and recreation? Or do you give in to the demands of others because of the intense needs around you?

This is a particular challenge for many pastors, missionaries, and anyone in the helping professions such as doctors, nurses, social workers, therapists, etc. We know the need is so great, and sometimes we feel like people's lives depend on us. This is why it is so important to not just learn to set healthy limits, but to learn to hear God's voice in all of this. I know there are times when I have to say no, but there are times when, even when I am tired, I feel God urging me to press on. There is no hard and fast rule. Healthy boundaries are always flexible.

As you saw in this chapter, Jesus' perspective is so different and freeing. He also clearly put me in my place and reminded me who the real Savior is!! I cry every time I read that story!

The book *Boundaries* by Townsend and Cloud can be extremely helpful if this is an area you are struggling with.

CHAPTER 17

With Joy Comes Grief

April 17, 2013 – Surprised by Sadness

I have been meeting regularly with Anne, one of my Uruguayan "sisters," the last few weeks to intentionally build joy between us. We adopted each other as family a few years back and have so enjoyed our friendship that we decided to strengthen it as much as possible before her first baby is born in just a few months.

We agreed to spend 5 minutes in silence together each time we see each other. During our silence, we look at each other for brief moments and then look away. It is sort of an adult version of peek-a-boo that I learned from our Thrive leadership training. It sounds bizarre, I know, but I have intentionally been enjoying my family this way now for a few months, and I can almost see our resilience growing week by week. Our trust is increasing and we feel glad to be together most of time. Our "normal" is not stressed and heavy anymore, but more and more it is tender, joyful, and light.

I have to say, however, I was not prepared for how deeply this time with my friend would impact me. On Monday, I felt a sadness stir during our time in silence looking at each other.

Flashes of four of my closest friends came to mind, all friends whom I left behind in the United States when I came to Uruguay.

Then today, this sadness settled in, and I began to feel like there were weights pressing in on my chest. I was driving down the road when it hit me. I knew I needed someone with me in it. I asked Jesus where He was and felt Him right beside me in the car. I looked over to the passenger seat and smiled. He was okay with my sadness. I could cry and just take my tears with me today. Then I sensed Him say, "Call Anne."

I pulled over, dialed her number, and as soon as I heard her voice, the tears overflowed.

"I am sad today." I barely got the words out.

"Oh, my sweet friend, that's okay. I'm here," Anne replied. She didn't need to change me, fix me, or stop me. She was happy to be with me even though I was sad. I felt strength come over me, like Popeye after eating spinach. The tears came, but I was not alone, and they were welcome.

"Thank you for being here," I said, ready to hang up and drive.

"Anytime. I love you." I could tell she was smiling.

I still do not know where all of this is coming from, but I trust the process.

April 18, 2013 – The Freedom to Mourn

I am randomly reading a journal that I found in the garage today dated 1990! The contents have undone me. It is like a water faucet has been turned on from deep within and hurt and grief are pouring out of it.

The journal tells of my best friend Pamela and the summer she, Matt, and I spent almost every day together working, playing, hanging out, and attending church as often as the door was open. We were partners on a mission trip, and probably because of that common experience, we began journaling about everything that was happening to us and between us. Many nights we would spend hours sharing and reading our journal entries to each other.

But by the end of the summer, she had fallen in love and had become engaged to an older guy we had met while working at the country club. He came from quite a different family with different means and thought it best for her to separate herself from us. So without warning, she was gone out of my life from one day to the next. The worst part for me was that he even demanded that she burn her journals that we had shared together… and she complied.

I was devastated and shocked. I had lost her, another best friend gone. But it happened so quickly that I just went on with my life. I was 17, in love with Matt, and busy preparing for college. I just closed the door and walked away.

But now, feeling so loved by my sweet friend/sister here, somehow I feel strong enough to mourn, and I just cry and cry, missing not only my lost friend from long ago, but all of my friends that I left 16 years ago by coming to Uruguay.

Images of Matt from that summer and all of my friends' faces come into focus and a smile surprises me. There are good feelings going on inside, as well. I feel precious and wanted. So often I only remember the bad things that have happened to me. But this is good. This is new for me. I am feeling desired and precious as I think about my friendships of old.

I extend my hands to receive all that my Lord and these memories have to give me. I want to let the good in and let it go deep into my soul.

May 2013 - Overwhelmed

I feel overwhelmed right now. The financial and emotional needs are taking me down. There is so much I want to do, but my own weak body limits me. I breathe and see Jesus holding me in the garden where we walk together sometimes. Sensing my stress, He pauses, leans in, and kisses my head.

"Toni, My precious, I love you so much. Even when you are

weak, I love you," He says as He looks into my eyes.

It still surprises me that He can love me when I am weak, when I cannot yet do so. I still do not want to accept my weakness, because accepting it means I have to grieve the loss of all that I want to do and accomplish. It amazes me how slow we humans are to learn. I spend so much time fighting what I need to accept. It is energy draining.

"I have such special plans for you, My child," He speaks directly to my thoughts. "We will do great things together. But they will not be done because you are strong." He smiles a compassionate, knowing smile.

"Patience. Rest in Me. Most of the stuff you want to get done does not matter. It just makes you feel more in control. But you are not in control. Continue fighting, but do not fight accepting what is true. You must accept, grieve, and fight to rest and to receive. That is your work right now."

"Okay," I say, somewhat defeated, as I lean my head into His chest and close my eyes. I do not want to hear these words. I want to hear that I am invincible and that with God nothing is impossible. But this is not what that verse means. And in the truth, there is a freedom that is so appealing. I can rest? We will do great things together while I am resting?

A sense of surrender and relief washs over me. I am important, protected, safe. I am calmed and soothed and want to offer this resting place to my husband and children. I also want to receive from them all of the love they give. May I grieve, rest, and receive.

CHAPTER 17

For Personal Reflection and Practice

1. Do an experiment this week: focus on enjoying those around you by naturally making eye contact a little more often and for a little longer than usual. Notice any changes in these relationships and the environment as a whole. When I did this, I noticed that my children were looking for my eyes all of the time, and I had never even realized it! They crave to be "seen" and want our eyes on them all of the time! My teen got embarrassed a little but liked it. My husband and I sent sparks all over the room without even realizing it! People told us to "get a room" just from our glances at each other!

2. As you build joy, pay attention to other emotions that can surface as well. Sometimes sadness hits me, and if I do not stop to reflect, I won't know it is there. What I *feel* is a desire to eat more or sleep more. Sadness makes me incredibly tired. These are my "cues" that I am sensing sadness and that I need to seek comfort in a healthy way by being with God and/or calling a friend. What are your cues? What do you normally do when you are sad?

Getting Back the Good

June 16, 2013 – My Sister

Yesterday was incredibly significant for me. Last week, I had written my sister a letter asking her to participate in an initiation ceremony that I wanted to do for my oldest daughter turning 13. I had no idea, but the letter actually slightly offended her.

My sister wrote me a beautiful email sharing how she felt when she read my letter and seeking clarification about what I was really trying to say. This moved me deeply because, in my past, people did not normally seek clarification when they were hurt by me. They just shamed me or isolated themselves so they did not get hurt again.

But this was different. My sister loved me enough to share with me her feelings, to make herself vulnerable to me. And she did it in such a mature, healing sort of way. Of course, I felt a little ashamed that I had hurt her, but I felt so loved at the same time.

I called her to talk about the letter and clarify things. Our conversation was incredibly healing for me. I experienced such grace coming from her and could not help but cry out of relief that she had not rejected me.

Hanging up the phone, I felt led to sit with my Creator and ask about the complex feelings I was feeling. As I let them come, I began crying like a little baby. I felt a pull coming from my diaphragm sucking my stomach and my chest together. The words "I receive my sister" came into my mind so loudly that I opened my hands and began rocking and saying them out loud over and over again. "I receive my sister. I receive my sister."

Then suddenly, an image of my sister hugging me close to her chest appeared. I was maybe 8 or 9. She seemed very concerned for me. She comforted me and protected me. I can tell by the look on her face I had been hurt, and she was like a mama bear gathered around her cub.

I know that my sister loves me. I know that she loved me back then. But this was the first time I had ever had a memory of being loved by her. How can it be that all of my life that memory was there in the recesses of my mind, and I never felt its presence? Maybe I am making this up. Maybe it never happened.

I accept it as true and receive it. I start crying and smiling at the same time. My sister really did love me. It is amazing to close my eyes and feel her protectively holding me.

I wonder if the joy I am experiencing in my present relationships is allowing my brain to connect to memories that had been somewhat lost before. I feel like I am getting back the good that happened to me as a child. I really am returning to JOY.

June 26, 2013 – Protected

I just arrived in the States, and before I did anything else, I had to talk to my sister, to ask her if she ever remembers holding and protecting me.

"Well, of course," she began. "It happened every time you got in trouble with Dad. I would hold you until you stopped crying. And yes, I wanted to protect you from him, and I usually was angry at him."

Tears flowed as I walked over and hugged my sister. I told her how sorry I was that I could never feel how much she loved me until now. I thanked her for her arms around me all those years and for being willing to share her feelings with me now. I told her how much she means to me. And how feeling loved and precious to others is new for me, but I am learning to let it in. It is new to receive like this, to let myself feel precious. It is awkward and uncomfortable, but it is so life-giving.

June 28, 2013 – I am Toni, Precious One

We are on vacation at a Christian family camp. The welcome already had me in tears as the camp counselors cheered us all the way from the entry to the front door of our hotel room! It almost felt like arriving in heaven and being greeted by all the saints who have gone before us. At least, coming from the spiritually dry land of Uruguay, that is how I felt on arrival!

During this morning's worship service, I had a pretty amazing, unsolicited, and unexpected encounter with my Lord. The praise band began with a new song I had never heard before by Meredith Andrews called "Not for a Moment." As the song unfolded, images began to emerge and play in my heart and mind.

My mom was there in my imagination, 21 years old and pregnant with me. I could see her long brownish-red hair and pale skin. She was happily interacting with others. I felt myself inside her tummy warm and safe. I could even feel her rubbing my little body through her stomach. Is this possible that I could have a physical memory of this? I don't know. Curious, I asked God, "What is this? What do You want me to know?"

"You are Toni, my precious one. You are precious." The words form in my mind and begin working in my soul. I lean into the memory and continue listening. "I have not left you alone, nor abandoned you. I put you in the right family. Even then, I was

172

there."

It is so strange how these words, even as I am writing them can feel so empty, and yet, when they were spoken in that moment, from within the depths of my soul, I felt deeply treasured and loved. These were not just words. These were words in the flesh, in action penetrating my heart, mind, and experience.

The song continued, and I saw my mom holding me after I was born. She looked so young, so beautiful. She was smiling at me and enjoying me. I was precious to her. This means so much to me because she does not have many memories or stories of what she enjoyed about me when I was little. I think most young moms are in so much trauma that our brains wipe out many of our memories, if we are not intentional about keeping them.

As I began to cry with feeling so enjoyed by my mother, I sensed God say, "Even then I did not forsake you. It was no accident that you were born to this family. I was not ignorant to this happening. I was there."

The song continued and images of some of my most difficult moments in life were brought forth. I saw myself being carried by Him through them all. I physically felt held, enjoyed, and cherished. This joy of feeling loved at such deep levels, was so overwhelmingly good, that I just stood and cried throughout the entire song. Past, present, future all seemed to run together as I felt held and seen and enjoyed by my mom and my Creator all at the same time. Physically, emotionally, spiritually, and intellectually, I sense I am being integrated, made whole.

I used to live being told I was loved, yet still feeling unloved inside or emotionally alone. This felt divided and crazy-making. Now, I am actually physically and emotionally *feeling* the truth that I am precious to my friends, my family, and my Creator. It is a huge difference.

People say the distance from your head to your heart is just eighteen inches, but the difference from my head to my "heart" has been a lifetime of experiencing God's presence rewriting the faulty mental scripts the broken world forged into my soul. We cannot convince ourselves of God's truth, we must experience and encounter His perspective in order for our minds to be made whole again. We can surrender to Him and receive from Him. And it is through relationship with Him that we will be made whole.

CHAPTER 18

For Personal Reflection and Practice

Sometimes music helps bypass the blocks we have to sensing God's presence and allows us to experience Him in new ways.

1. Ask yourself and God what kind of music you need most today. Maybe you need Hymns, maybe contemporary praise and worship, maybe love songs from the 80's (if you are like me!).

2. Play whatever music you feel like your soul needs most right now.

3. Close your eyes and let the words come to life in your imagination. Give your imagination to God, and ask Him to show you what these songs look like for you and Him. How is this song like your relationship with Him? How is it different? Enter into a playful space where you can interact freely with yourself and God without judging. Write down all that you experience and how you feel during the song.

4. Share with someone who won't think you are crazy!

Appreciation, God's Way Back to Joy

August 11, 2013 – From Hopeless Despair to Joy

I come to You in hopeless despair, oh my God. First of all, we have never been in this much financial need. You have always provided for us. Why are You not providing right now?

Secondly, since arriving back in Uruguay three weeks ago from our second year of Thrive training, it has been one crisis after the other in our community here. The first week back, we were in the emergency room with our precious little premature Uruguayan niece. The following week, we were in the emergency room with the caretaker from San Geronimo, who is still in ICU. And right now, I just received a message that my Uruguayan nephew has gone into the emergency room for self-harm and suicidal tendencies.

That is all on top of the stress of having been gone for a month, and the grief of leaving my birth family behind again. I'm living without the resources I need to live well. I need other people to enjoy my children and play with them. How can they thrive with so little joy around them and so much crisis?

I miss watching my brother-in-law play with my kids. He has such a gift for play, and they enjoyed him so much and felt so loved by him and my sister. I miss all the love and attention that my mom and dad gave them, as well. Here in Uruguay, I am mother, aunt, cousin, grandparent, teacher and therapist for my kids. I cannot be everything for them. I need people who not only love and want to be with my kids, but who have the extra time and energy to pour into them. We have worked so hard to build a beautifully healthy family here in Uruguay, but everyone's resources are overtaxed. Just living each day here is enough to suck each person dry. There is no room for margin like in the United States.

I feel empty and broken, so hopeless. And yet somehow, I'm supposed to pull it all together to play with my children, see their emotional needs, and enjoy them.

All the hospital visits and caring for our community has exhausted me. Our entire community is in trauma. How do we hold on to each other and to You in the midst of this?

Leaving my family to come to Uruguay was much easier the first 10 years or so because I was running away and escaping a dysfunctional system. However, God has healed and changed all of us so much over the last three years that they are now a huge source of joy for me. While I am so thankful for God's restoration, it unfortunately means that leaving them has become very painful.

"Spend time in appreciation, Toni," I hear. "Tell Me how it felt when you were watching your kids being enjoyed by your family in the States?" I sense this is God responding to me, seeing me, guiding me.

As I remember their play times, a smile comes instantly to my face. Tension leaves my shoulders as I share my memory with Jesus. "I felt rested. I felt so thankful that my precious kiddos were being enjoyed and that it did not have to come from me. I felt not alone. There was no tension in my shoulders, no tension anywhere. And I was smiling and laughing a lot."

"Write a letter to your brother-in-law and your sister telling them how much you appreciate their involvement in the life of your children." Jesus is teaching me how to get unstuck from hopeless despair. He is showing me that the resources that are within my own heart, my joy memories, are indeed powerful! Remembering these moments brings the lightness to my heart even in the midst of the chaos of this morning. I smile, laugh, and relax as I give myself to this life-giving task.

August 21, 2013 – Hurting, Yet Peaceful

Papa, these last four days have seen their share of stress and pressure. The financial shortage is overwhelming. Matt and I just cry together many nights wondering what to do. You have always provided for us. Please show us what our part is in this ordeal.

My mom called me this morning to say that my dad went in for emergency, open heart, triple-bypass surgery. Thank You, thank You for saving his life! Thank You that he realized he was in pain, went to the hospital, and that they started surgery before the heart attack was able to take his life. He is recovering well.

I turn to appreciation, to memories. You've told me to remember, remember, and remember. I remember feeling loved by my sister. I think of You saving my dad's life, and I remember the tender moment my mom, dad, and I shared in the middle of the parking lot just weeks ago when I was home.

"Mom, Dad," I said as we were walking from the car to the store, "I want you to know that I draw so much strength from you still to this day. Even though I live so far away, I want you to know that your enjoyment of me helps me endure. I could not do it without you."

They both stopped and turned toward me, surprised at what I was saying.

I looked both of them in the eyes and said, "The fact that you enjoy me is monumental, and I want you to know how much I appreciate you in my life."

They both put their arms around me, sandwiching me between them. "We do enjoy you," they said. "And we love you very much!"

We lingered, holding each other and crying, right there in the parking lot. Then we burst into laughter at the thought of what we must have looked like to all the other customers going shopping that day!

With each memory, I draw closer to God Himself. I can feel His compassion for my despair and my doubt. He wants me to be so close to Him that He is bigger than all of my problems.

I remember what my Thrive training has taught me: If I am distressed, I probably am not sensing God's presence with me. But when I am hurting and yet peaceful, then I know I am aware that God is here.

August 28, 2013 – Carried Along

I come to You today completely exhausted. An image comes to mind of You carrying me along the beach. I have sensed that You won't leave me behind even when I am too tired to go on. You lovingly scoop me up and carry me wherever You want me to be. And I get to just rest in Your arms. I sense You leading me to sleep. I will go and rest with You.

September 1, 2013 – Isaiah 55

I woke up this morning at 4am feeling awake and alert. As I was trying to go back to sleep, I heard the words, "Come" in my head. "Come be with Me." I sensed an invitation from Jesus. It has been years since this has happened in the wee hours of the morning. Usually, I gobble up every second of sleep I can.

This morning, however, a sneaky smile came over me, and I quickly got up, put on my robe, and crept quietly to the living room, Bible and journal in hand.

I decided to reflect on Isaiah 55 because it was an assignment from the Forming study I am doing. It is one of the Connexus classes from Life Model Works. So, sensing Jesus with me, I pulled out the passage and began reading. An image came to mind, and as I paid attention to it, it became an interactive story in my imagination. I went with it, asking questions along the way to myself and to God. Below is what unfolded.

"Hey, everyone who thirsts, come to the waters; and you who have no money, come, buy and eat!" (my paraphrase, vs. 1a).

I see a girl running through the woods, running for her survival. Panicked, hot, and tired, bow and arrow strapped to her back, she seems somewhat desperate as she comes upon a clearing and a brook. Looking around to make sure there are no enemies, she cautiously moves to the water, throws down her weapons, falls to her knees, and drinks. As she drinks freely, she notices across the way someone is selling food to people who have no money.

"This is strange… not right," she reasons. How can someone "Come, buy and eat" when they have "no money"? What *is* she to pay with if not money? Her soul? Her humility? Her need? Her desperate state? She is hesitant to trust. It looks like a scam, a trap. It seems too good to be true.

"Come, buy wine and milk without money, without price," she hears again (vs. 2b).

She is tempted. She longs to be fed. She is so hungry, and she knows she will die without food. She walks over, makes eye contact with the seller, and tentatively takes the bread he is handing her. Before she realizes what is happening, she has backed away and is hunched over her food, ravaging it protectively like an animal, her eyes staying focused on Him.

Is He for real? Can He be trusted? Her mind is searching for answers to explain what is happening. She examines His eyes for what seems like minutes. They seem tender. They seem real and sincere.

He breaks the silence. "Why do you spend your money on what is not bread? And your labor for that which does not satisfy?" (vs. 2a). His question does not sound condemning, but compassionate, invitational.

She begins to think about this. What have I spent my money on? What has made me so poor, yet running so hard? Memories flash into her mind of spending herself for the affection of others. She has worked hard to deserve being loved, only to still be in debt. She has spent herself trying to meet others' needs so that they would like her... so that she would like herself. She is only valuable if she can give, right? Yet, she is so tired and hungry. She wants to receive. She wants to feel loved. She wants to feel valued just because she is.

"Listen carefully to me," He says as she continues feasting. She has never had food so satisfying and water so refreshing. He has her attention. She pauses from eating to listen.

"Eat what is good, and delight yourselves in rich food," He says as He shows the abundance He has before Him (vs. 2b). She realizes for the first time she is not alone. Others have come as well, tired and worn, but there is enough for all of them to eat. She looks around and hears Him whisper to her, "Stop scraping for the scraps of acceptance and love, validation, and worth that fall at others' feet. Instead, come, pull up a chair, and let Me delight in you. My enjoying you is rich food, good and satisfying, and there is plenty to feast on. Sit down and have a meal. You are worth that and so much more to Me."

Once seated, the wine is poured and He begins again. "Incline your ear to Me and come to me; hear, that your soul may live" (vs. 3a). "For as the rain and the snow come down from heaven and do not return there but water the earth, making it bring forth and sprout, giving seed to the sower and bread to the eater, so shall my word be that goes out from my mouth; it shall not return to me empty, but it shall accomplish that which I purpose, and shall succeed in the thing for which I sent it. For you shall go out in joy and be led forth in peace; the mountains and the hills before you shall break forth into singing, and all the trees of the field shall clap their hands." (vs. 10-12).

He can see that she does not quite understand and begins again, "Now that you are feasting on My love for you, My enjoyment of you, My deep affection for you, My validation of you, listen intently to Me so that you will live, truly live. Once you are here feasting on My love for you, then I will speak to you words that will change you. They will be so profound, I guarantee they will transform your heart so that you will walk into your world with joy, knowing I am so delighted to be with you no matter what. And I will lead you out in peace. Your thoughts will no longer be racing to and fro trying to find the crumbs left over from others. No, you will go in peace, quieted, knowing there is plenty here for you when you need it. Knowing I am here, waiting for you to come."

The third person story ends here, and I become the girl. I want to bring all of the different facets of me to this abundant table. I am in. He has earned my trust. I call on all of my wounded self to come…

The little girl who lost her best friend at 8 years old, *come*.

The little sister who felt rejected, *come*.

The little girl who didn't get to ride the roller coaster, *come*.

The little girl neglected by her father, *come*.

The little girl who felt left out, *come*.

The teenager who wanted to feel precious to someone, to anyone, *come*.

The young missionary dying for recognition, *come*.

The young wife, chronically exhausted and unseen, *come*.

The mother, empty and lonely, *come*.

There is food, good food, rich food! Feast on His attention toward you, on how much He longs to be with you. Enjoy.

"We are all here, my Lord," I say as I take inventory of the wounded parts of me. "Oh wait, there is one more…"

Come, beautiful woman scared to death that the pressure will never end. Mad that God is not acting like you think He should. Afraid that He will not give you what you need...

Jesus, knowing my thoughts, leans in and responds. "All you really need is joy and peace – My words whispered to you at My table as we eat together, as you let Me enjoy you. Let… Me… enjoy you…" He gently implores.

He takes me in His arms and carries me to a beach. The air is perfect, the sun setting. I nuzzle in and rest. It has been a long time since I have slept safe and sound. After what seems like days of being carried, He stops and sets me down at an elegantly prepared table for two right there overlooking the ocean, sand beneath our feet. It has a white tablecloth and is set for a meal. I am confused. He motions for me to sit and have a private dinner with Him. I can't take my eyes off of Him as He gently helps me into my seat and then finds His own.

He takes my hands in His and looks at me intently. I feel a little embarrassed at first. I am not used to receiving this much attention, to being seen. But it feels honoring, special.

"Yes?" I finally break the silence out of discomfort.

"You are my precious, Toni. I have loved you since the moment time began… no, since before time began. I have waited for this day for so long."

I am confused. Could He really love ME this much? I hold His gaze testing His eyes for truth. Flashes of Him wooing me, loving me, protecting me, healing me over the course of my lifetime appear through my mind.

"I have waited for this moment for thousands of years," He says as He looks me in the eyes, kisses my cheek, and then my forehead. Tears come. Could I possible be this important to Him?

I feel like I am truly meeting Him for the first time. I have sensed Him so often, even seen Him, but something is different now. He is creating a place for us to come and be together whenever I need Him, a place to abide in with Him.

"Come, dance with Me," He says with a smile as He offers His hand.

Dumbfounded, I accept His invitation. We move to the dry sand, and as we dance I am soothed, quieted, my fears and doubts drifting to the background.

Knowing my heart, He whispers in my ear, "Do you think I am going to let you down?"

His question brings tears to my eyes, as I am reminded of my fears. "I don't know what to think anymore, Lord."

"Trust Me. Trust this," He says as He lifts our enveloped hands to my eyes, showing me our togetherness. "I will take care of you," He promises emphatically.

"But what about our economic situation? What about our missional business? What about San Geronimo?"

"Leave it with Me and trust Me," He says again and twirls me around playfully. This playfulness irritates me slightly because I still feel so heavy.

Then it occurs to me that He is not feeling heavy.

"You're not afraid, are you?" I ask in disbelief. He is peaceful, calm, even playful in the midst of all that is going on.

"No, I am not afraid, My love," He begins. "I am working! There is so much going on here that you do not see." He drops my hands and breaks away excited to tell me all about it. "I am training. I am building. I am preparing. I am opening hearts and minds. I am bringing My Kingdom into this world through you all, and you don't even realize it! It is a battle, but it is already won!"

He moves in close again and takes my hands and looks me in the eyes. "Look to Me in the midst of it, and you will see My peace. I am not afraid. I have already won!"

We begin to dance again. My whole body tingles all over as I feel His cheek on mine and contemplate His words. I am satisfied and quieted.

He whispers again in my ear, "You are precious to Me. I love you. I won't let anything hurt you. Trust Me. No one can take My enjoying you away from you."

I give myself fully to the dance, to Him. I feel confident that He is with me. There is strength in the midst of my utter weakness. I play, and I rest, and I trust.

CHAPTER 19

For Personal Reflection and Practice

I invite you to do the following guided meditative exercise from Isaiah 55. I have included the verses for your convenience and the questions intermixed below. Find a quiet place with at least 30 to 40 minutes of uninterrupted time and enjoy!

"Hey, everyone who thirsts, come to the waters; and you who have no money, come, buy and eat!"(vs. 1a)

I invite you to imagine yourself thirsty, hungry and at the end of your rope. What does that look like for you? What images come to mind?

What does it feel like to be needy?

What is it you are thirsty and hungry for?

"Come, buy wine and milk without money, without price," (vs. 2b).

You hear the call again. Imagine this invitation being made directly to you. What do you pay with? What, if not money, are you supposed to "buy" with? Are you hesitant to trust this "free" food? If so, why?

"Why do you spend your money on what is not bread? And your labor for that which does not satisfy" (vs. 2a)?

What have you spent your money on? What has made you so poor, yet running so hard? What have you spent yourself on?

What is it you need? What do you want? Do you approach and take the food offered? What does that look like in your imagination?

"Listen carefully to me, eat what is good, and delight yourselves in rich food, (vs. 2b)"

What could God be whispering to you right now? What is your invitation to? What exactly is His rich food you are to delight in?

"Incline your ear to Me and come to me; hear, that your soul may live" (vs. 3a). "For as the rain and the snow come down from heaven and do not return there but water the earth, making it bring forth and sprout, giving seed to the sower and bread to the eater, so shall my word be that goes out from my mouth; it shall not return to me empty, but it shall accomplish that which I purpose, and shall succeed in the thing for which I sent it. For you shall go out in joy and be led forth in peace; the mountains and the hills before you shall break forth into singing, and all the trees of the field shall clap their hands" (vs. 10-12).

What does this passage look like in your imagination?

Pay attention to any images that have come to you during this time. Ask Jesus if there is anything He wants you to know? How does He feel about being with you?

CHAPTER 20

Living into a New Reality

September 5, 2013 – Appreciating All Together

It has been an absolutely wonderful week. How my time with You in Isaiah has changed me! I have more energy than normal and feel centered. Matt and I have been sensing You with us, as well, guiding us in fund raising.

What is different? I try to live in our place on the beach. I am in Your arms dancing, and You are holding me close. That feels so true and real that it eclipses our problems. They do not feel unmanageable or hopeless.

Then, in my imagination, sometimes Matt appears and comes to me on the beach. I am standing in the surf admiring Your beauty in the sunset over the horizon, and Matt appears beside me admiring me. And there we are, me appreciating You and him appreciating me. The fact that I feel seen and appreciated by him is amazing and a sign of just how much we both are growing individually and together.

September 21, 2013 – Staying in Appreciation

Learning to receive means staying in appreciation. Finding the moments when I am fully present and bringing all of my senses into that moment.

Yesterday, I was walking hand-in-hand into the mall with my precious three-year-old boy. His hand felt warm and small inside mine. I became fully aware of how much I enjoy him and how quickly he will be gone. I smiled as my fullness culminated in tears. I told him how much I loved him, how much I enjoyed him. He got so excited that he started hopping just like a bunny into the mall entrance. I laughed, not caring what everyone around me thought, and began hopping right along with him.

Then today, I was brushing my youngest daughter's hair. I usually rush right through it trying to get to wherever we're going. But today, as I held her hair in my hands, time stopped for the moment. I slowed down and enjoyed each stroke down her golden locks. Her beauty expanded my soul, and I was in awe of her precious, little life. As I quietly thanked God that I get to be her mommy, tears came, and I could feel the Divine present and enjoying both of us. He is so satisfied that I am trying to fully enjoy the amazing gifts He has given me.

Receiving also means appreciating God. As I turn my mind and heart toward Him, I see us there enjoying our dinner for two on the beach and then dancing. After some time, we move to a blanket to watch the sun set together. I am cuddled between His legs and His arms are around me as I lean into His chest.

"You have become my Lover," I say out loud. "Not in a sexual way, but in a very intimate way. I am overwhelmed with how gently You care for me. How You don't mind that I am weak. How You see something so amazing in me that I can't even see myself. You're one of the very few who really sees inside of me. Thank You for this. Thank You for going at my pace, for attuning to my emotions."

Time slows when I'm with Him and I rest. I don't have to be

there for Him. I don't have to *do* for Him. He doesn't need me to be anyone but who I am. It is life-giving. It is like coming in out of the cold after a long journey and finding a fire made and food on the table ready to be eaten.

"Is there anything else You want me to know about this moment?" I ask as I bask in His presence, enjoying the sunset in my imagination.

Slowly, I notice something being washed up on the shore. I stand and go to investigate. It is money! Money is washing up on the shore!

"Is this image from You? Or am I just imposing my own dreams?" I turn and ask. He does not answer, but playfully stands, as if He is going to tackle me. We start to play fight. I try to tickle Him and then run. He chases after me, laughing. I turn and toss sand back at Him as I go. All the while, the money continues to wash up on the shore.

> Lover of my heart,
> How can You see into me?
> My eyes dare not drift from Your face.

> Lover of my soul,
> How can You not fear in a time like this?
> Discouragement lingers near.

> Lover of my mind,
> How can You know the way out of the dark?
> Do not let my hand slip from Yours. Lead me.

September 25, 2013 – I Will Take Care of You

I am amazed at the new relationship I have found with my Creator, my Savior, my Lover. Every day, I wake up feeling overwhelmed with the current circumstances of our life. But as I go in my imagination to the images You have given me, You bring rest to my soul. It is much better than escaping into a novel. This is my story, and it is just as intriguing as the best of novels. It is like escaping into *true* reality instead of escaping *from* reality!

I am here now, dancing with You. Your presence immediately draws out my fears.

"I am so scared," I say out loud.

"I will take care of you," You whisper into my ear, reminding me You have not left me alone.

Help me believe, oh, my Lord. Feeling Your physical body close to mine – holding me, dancing with me – relaxes my whole body. Your heartbeat has the power to slow mine down. Renewing my mind is not merely memorizing Scripture and quoting it to myself to try to change my emotional reality. There is no relationship in that. Renewing my mind is coming to You, interacting with You, feeling You close, and letting You speak Your truth to my inner places. You are the Living Word, and as I quiet in Your presence, You whisper Your Word to me.

"Fear not, for I am with you; be not dismayed, for I am your God" (Isaiah 41:10).

"Come to me all who labor and are heavy laden, and I will give you rest" (Matthew 11:28).

I come. I linger. I dance. You lead. I am not afraid.

October 1, 2013 – Out of Control

There are so many things out of my control that I do not like, and I don't want to accept them. Dysfunctional relationships around me, my oldest not following God, chronic financial shortage, the broken car, the broken water pipes, the broken refrigerator, not being able to be in the States to support my niece and her new baby, not being able to be with my premature Uruguayan grand-niece because of necessary health precautions,

I don't want to accept these things. Help me see Your perspective, Father.

I sense You, at the table on the beach, listening and holding my hands as I speak. You see that I am stressed, that my mind is swirling around, that I'm almost making myself nauseous by my inability to accept my current circumstances.

You look into my eyes and say, "I love you, you know. Even when you are like this."

Tears start to flow, and I look away.

"Let go. Feel the pain and mourn the losses. It will not be more than we can handle together." You stand up, pull me to my feet, and begin to dance with me. I realize this is a type of quieting together. It is amazing to me how You get inside of me and calm the storms. In Your arms, I feel at peace and deeply loved. Tears flow. I can accept because I can grieve.

October 3, 2013 – You Work with Me

John 14:1 says, "Let not your hearts be troubled. Believe in God; believe also in me."

My heart has been troubled this week. I have been hounded by hopeless thoughts. "I am nobody. I could have been someone great had I not come to Uruguay. But now I have no credentials, and no reason for people to even listen to me. I will never do public speaking or use my communication gifts. I have wasted away by going to 'the ends of the earth.'"

I sense You draw close to me, take me to our table at the beach, and speak Your truth right to the core of my soul. "I let you enter into people's lives and watch Me transform them. I have uniquely gifted you to put people's hands into Mine. You get to work with Me! Is that not enough for you?"

"Yes," I say with tears streaming down my face. His admonishment feels freeing, not punishing. "Yes, my Creator."

My worth is not in my fame, in how many churches I plant, or how many people I have helped, but in being His and being with Him. My story of Him in my life is my treasure. I need to be faithful to write it.

October 4, 2013 – I am Not Alone

I have been working through the Forming course, and the exercises that it has for us to do are so amazingly helpful for engaging with You, my Jesus.

Today, I am to meditate on Psalm 139:1-6:

O Lord, you have searched me and known me!
You know when I sit down and when I rise up;
you discern my thoughts from afar.
You search out my path and my lying down
and are acquainted with all my ways.
Even before a word is on my tongue,
behold, O Lord, you know it altogether.
You hem me in, behind and before,
and lay your hand upon me.
Such knowledge is too wonderful for me;
it is high; I cannot attain it.

As I ask my Lord what this looks like in my life, quick flashes of me throughout my day fill my mind. Images come of me brushing my teeth, sleeping, getting frustrated with the kids, cooking, cleaning, etc. But as these images surface like pictures, I see that He is right there beside me in each one. The reality hits that I am never alone, never. He is always at my side watching me, seeing me, noticing me, wanting me.

One of the biggest gaps in my maturity as a child was that I did not feel seen. It is like God himself is re-parenting me and giving me everything I did not get as a child.

The image of Him as the Father, the Son, and the Holy Spirit surrounding me, protecting me, comes to mind again.

"Why do You love me so?" I ask. "I still cannot understand it. I am nothing."

"You are *not* nothing! You are MINE!" He almost yells, then quietly adds, "And I think you are fascinating."

I don't feel very fascinating. And it doesn't seem to me that others find me fascinating. Not many want to know what goes on inside of me. I'm too much for people to handle.

"You are not too much for Me to handle," He interrupts my pity party. "Let Me give you what you have been missing. Let Me be with you all day. I long to know every one of your thoughts."

As He says this, I feel indebted to Him, and thankful, and grateful. Maybe I overwhelm people with all that is inside of me because I need to be seen so badly. Maybe if *He* sees me, I won't need from other people as much, and maybe I won't overwhelm them anymore. I will be able to contain myself more and protect others from feeling overwhelmed with all the emotions that go on inside of me. Hope comes in. And I begin to see a different way forward, slowly, but surely.

December 2, 2013 – Doing What I Want

So often I only see what I don't get to do in life. The other day I sensed God inviting me to see a different reality, one that was much lighter and joy-filled.

I was at the end of a full day, exhausted. I had played with my kids, trained them, helped them through their daily emotional crises, and I was exhausted. I had hoped to have some time for "me" that day – time to quilt, to read, or even to work – but it had been impossible.

As I lay in bed that night, my thoughts raced, "I didn't get to do anything I wanted to do today." Sadness accompanied these thoughts.

Then the simple question came, "But, Toni, didn't you want to take care of your family today?"

"Yes, I did want to care for my family today," I replied curiously.

"Then you did what you wanted to do, right?"

I laughed out loud and a smile claimed my face. I am so thankful I got to take care of my children today. I was the one who got to train them, play with them, and get them unstuck emotionally. I did not have to leave them with someone else.

Thank You, Papa that I get to be a full-time mom for them. They are so worth my time, and I am enjoying getting to know them. They will be gone in a blink of an eye, and it will be just my husband and me again. Thank You for helping me receive these beautiful gifts that You have given me. Thank You for helping me see that I am not a victim who cannot do what I want to do. But I make choices to do exactly what I want to do! And caring for my family is just that! This perspective feels like fresh air coming into a polluted environment. May it cleanse me of my victim mentality!

CHAPTER 20

For Personal Reflection and Practice

God wants us to learn to feel all of the more difficult emotions and still be able to sense His presence with us at the same time. That way, we are hurting and yet peaceful, instead of hurting and anxious, tense, stressed or depressed. As you see throughout this book, most of my imaginative work with God consists of moments where He is meeting me in a heavy emotion, such as shame, anger, sadness, fear, hopelessness or a combination of them all, and showing me that He is glad to be with me anyway! That is joy! His presence shows me that he is not afraid of my emotion or of my situation and, therefore, I do not have to be either.

1. Out of these emotions, shame, anger, sadness, fear, disgust, hopeless despair, which do you find it hardest to feel and still act like yourself? Which do you try to avoid feeling the most?

2. Next time you are ashamed, angry, sad, afraid, or feeling hopeless try to quiet yourself with deep breathing and scanning your body. Then, ask Jesus how He feels about being with you. Also, ask Him if there is anything you need to know about how you are feeling.

PART V

• • • • •

Learning to Suffer Well
(2013-2014)

The Invitation

October 2007

Just let me go back to sleep.
I was having this great dream
Isolated from the pain
Of modern man gone insane.

I was living in a world
Where babies don't cry,
Where children aren't abandoned
Where people don't lie.

It's easy to go to sleep
And ignore the need.
Just comfort my own soul
Leave others out in the cold

It's safer not to share
In their pain
Not to hear their cries
Not to see their lives

What would I miss
If I lived this way?
Being a hero?
Saving the day?

Helping the poor?
Making a dent in this horrific madness
Of a world
Filled with sadness?

A hero,
I don't need to be,
And saving the world is
Not all it's cracked up to be.

And yet, there is a story
I am invited to join.
I can watch one on TV
Or dive into the real one
I see all around me.

Then there's something to be said
For responsibility
We have not for ourselves,
for our comfort, for our sprees
We have so that we can give
So that others can live.

So I can't just go back to sleep.
Although it's a tempting idea
Not when there's an invitation
To live, to receive, and to give.

CHAPTER 21

The Man with the Sandwich

March 5, 2013 – Responding Well

Today, my entire family was affronted. We were returning from the airport with my parents who had just arrived from the States for a three-week visit. There was much laughter in the car. Our reunion had sparked story after story of what had happened in our lives in the last six months since we had seen each other. Turning the corner to our street, we saw another car pretty far away driving toward us. Our neighborhood streets only let one car pass at a time. As our house was just a few houses up on the left, I thought I could make the turn before the other car got to where we were.

Upon speeding up, however, I noticed that the other car sped up, as well. Maybe they were going to do the same thing, I thought, so I began to slow down to give them the way. But much to my surprise, the other car was not trying to turn anywhere, and before we could get to my house, the driver intentionally stopped his car directly in front of ours, nose to nose.

We had no idea what was happening. He did not look angry, but also did not make eye contact. In my confusion, I wondered if

I had offended this man somehow.

I was not sure what to do. And then, the man turned his car off, leaned over, got his lunch from the passenger's seat, stepped out of the car, closed his door, walked across to the grass, sat down, and nonchalantly began eating his sandwich as if nothing were happening.

Everyone in my car was dumbfounded. Why would someone treat us this way? I had no idea what was going on in this man's heart, but his actions felt abusive. My dad was in the passenger seat of the car, and I could tell he was fuming.

I quickly prayed, "Jesus help." I took a deep breath, and knowing that my dad did not speak the language and that he would probably let his anger get the best of the situation, I put my hand on his chest and said, "I'll take care of this."

I took my time getting out of the car. I brought to mind the memories of Jesus and me together on the beach. I sensed Jesus dancing with me, holding me. I took a deep breath. His words, "No one can ever take My enjoying you away from you," filled my heart and mind. I let the feeling of His cheek on my cheek calm all my anger and bring me out of my lizard brain into the place where I remember whose I am, and what it is like my people to do in situations like this. It is like us to bless those who curse.

I closed my car door calmly, and I walked over to where the man was sitting on the grass. He was definitely shocked that I would approach him with a smile on my face and warmth in my heart, but he just kept eating his sandwich.

I sat down beside him, and said in Spanish, "Sir, I'm wondering if I can pray for you today."

"What?" he replied.

I continued in all sincerity, "Yes, I would like to pray for you, because you see, I can only imagine you must be having a difficult day, and I would really like to pray for you."

The man didn't know what to say. He looked at me in shock. In Uruguay, aggressive actions are always met with anger and confrontation. Here I was a foreigner, and I was not yelling or confronting him, but actually showing him kindness when he deserved anger and hate.

"You can do whatever you want to," he said to me, "but leave me out of it."

I replied, "No, I think you actually need God today." He shrugged his shoulders apathetically.

I took a deep breath, placed my hand on his back, and asked Jesus to pray through me what this man needed. Surprisingly, even to myself, words flowed from my mouth in Spanish over this man. I heard myself begging God to bring him and his family to know the deep, abiding love of Jesus. I asked God to bless him with abundant joy and peace.

When I was done, I looked the man in the eyes, sincerely enjoying him as a deeply beloved creation of God. Standing to leave, I added, "I hope you have a really good day, sir."

He was stunned into silence.

Upon returning to my car, I could feel the adrenaline getting the best of me. My body was shaking all over. This had been a very painful experience, and while I had stayed relational, my body was carrying the consequences of having been sinned against. Is this what Peter referred to as being a "partner with Christ in His suffering" (1 Peter 4:13, NLT)?

I got back in the car and decided to go around the block to get to my house. By the time I turned the corner to our street, the man's car was gone.

"What did you say to him?" my parents wanted to know. They were angry and shocked. What a welcome this was to Uruguay!

I was still shaking all over and I knew, for my emotional health, that I needed to tell the story. As I recounted what had happened, I sensed God and others validating that what that man did was wrong and hurtful. They all looked at me in the eyes and assured me that I had done nothing wrong. I did not deserve to be treated that way.

I was able to cry and let my emotions come. At the same time, I felt God's pleasure over me for how I had responded to this man.

"You did not forget whose you are!" I sensed Jesus saying. "I want that man to know Me, and today he has experienced My love like never before in his entire life."

I am so satisfied with how I handled this today. It is not without a cost, but my community and God Himself came to my need and healed my wounds. While I am so sad that my parents were received into Uruguay that way, I am thankful they are here and that we are in God's hands.

CHAPTER 21

For Personal Reflection and Practice

1. In what ways do your emotions get the better of you? Have you ever done something like the man with the sandwich? Or, if you relate more to me in the story, how would you have responded?

2. What do you do when you find yourself out of control emotionally? How do you calm yourself down?

3. What skills have you learned throughout this book that might be useful for you to practice, so that in intense moments you have more control over your reactions?

CHAPTER 22

The Man on the Bike

March 9, 2013 – Compassionate Response

The other day, I was trying to park on the opposite side of the street, so I pulled into a driveway to turn around. A man nearby on a bicycle looked at me with accusing and contemptuous eyes as if I had done something illegal. I sank into my seat with the weight of shame. Without thinking, my mind was already calling on Jesus' name to guide and protect me. I felt Him near and instantly came out of my shame and into Jesus' perspective of what was happening.

"This man is filled with anger, Toni. It has nothing to do with you. He is bound by his own pain and is lashing out at you because you are weaker than he is."

This reality changed my perspective. I sensed compassion for the man and wanted to somehow bless him. I wanted him to know that I meant no harm, and that I was sorry I had inadvertently offended him. The quickest idea that came to mind was to wave at him and smile. So I did just that.

He looked even angrier, but thankfully, began to bike away. I parked, but my adrenalin was pumping, my heart was racing, and I was shaking all over. I tried to calm myself, but noticed that even as the man biked away, he continued to stare at me. I sensed fear rising in me. Trying again to communicate a heart of peace towards him, I waved and smiled as I got out of my car. Before I could enter the office building, the man turned his bike around and came back to where I was. I could see that he was not just angry but enraged.

I was completely aghast. I had done nothing wrong to earn this man's anger. I knew God would protect me emotionally and spiritually from anything, but I definitely feared for my physical safety. I quickly walked to the office and rang the doorbell, hoping that someone would open before the man could approach me.

He stopped ten feet away and whistled to detain me from entering the building. The door was still locked. I turned to face him. He began screaming at me, "Are you joking with me? Are you pulling my leg? You are so inconsiderate pulling into the driveway like that and now you're going to smile at me? What is wrong with you? Are you making fun of me?"

"No," I replied somewhat panicked. "I just really want you to have a good day today. I meant you no harm." As quickly as I could get the words out, the door opened, and I ran into the office, frantically closing the door behind me.

I was so taken aback and shaking all over, that I went to the bathroom and quieted my body with the Shalom for my Body exercises I had learned from the Thrive training. I cried a little and felt God's perspective wash over me, "Toni, you are ok now. You are safe. You were not in the wrong. I saw how unfair that was." My body was calmer and able to function, but thoughts were still bouncing all over. I got through my meeting and made it home.

Thankfully, we had a time of prayer scheduled that evening with my parents, Matt, and one of our teammates. During prayer, I felt that I needed to share with everyone what had happened and ask God what He wanted me to know about the incident.

As everyone prayed for me, I sensed Jesus holding me in the garden, where we sometimes go, saying, "I saw all of that, Toni. I am so sorry that happened to you. You need to cry it out. I am here." As I cried and cried, Jesus felt my pain, and looking into my eyes with compassion continued, "You responded well, My child. You need not fear going back."

What a relief! I had already begun to fear that place and dreaded returning. Now I felt safe to go back. Also, Jesus was pleased with me, with how I had responded with love. This felt deeply validating and exciting. It is proof that He really is changing me.

My mind began wondering why... why do these seemingly random things happen to me?

Understanding my thoughts, I sensed Jesus say, "There are people who need to have an encounter with Me. You tend to respond very differently than most people when you are hurt. You let Me act through you. I am using you in these moments. They will come, maybe more and more, but know it is in My plan. Your attackers will encounter Me through you. And know that I will be with you. Do not fear. I am so proud of you."

I cried and cried with my community around me. I felt validated, assured, valued, held, encouraged, and *healed*. Jesus' presence is so sweet. I remember sitting with Papa God, Jesus, and the Holy Spirit in my training last year. I remember feeling so indebted to my God, my Creator, that I asked Him what He wanted from me. I think He wants me to feel His joy and His presence with me even in the midst of attack, so that I can let Him respond and show others who He is.

"I am Yours, my God," I say, offering my life to Him. "If that is what it takes for someone to come to know Your love for them, here I am, send me."

CHAPTER 22

For Personal Reflection and Practice

In the majority of this book you have seen how Jesus is 100% about seeking and saving all that was lost inside of me, between us, and in my relationships with others. That means loving me deeply, meeting me were I am, giving me rest, restoring my soul, re-parenting me, and healing my trauma. He has proven Himself as my Good Shepherd, my Savior, my Lord, my King, my Papa, my Friend and my Lover.

Somehow, at the same time, Jesus is also about seeking and saving *all* that was lost in the world around me as well. As He restores me, He invites me to join Him in this incredible mission of harvesting His shalom in the world around me. Each of us is uniquely gifted for this purpose. Our gift is the unique way we bear His image.

Many times I run into mission because I think it is what I am "supposed to do" as a follower of Christ. Sometimes it is hard to stay in the resting/listening space until He knows I am ready to follow where He leads. While it does not *feel* productive to me, this space is so important because He resources me for what lies ahead.

1. Where are you in this whole process? Do you feel like you are just learning to receive and listen? Do you feel like you are practicing letting Him bring you back to joy from different emotions? Or can you readily sense Him in almost every moment, every emotion and every breath? Are you in a resourcing space or have you sensed Papa move you into mission in a given area?

2. While I tend to be on the "front lines," you will notice in these stories that I have a community to help repair what is hurt while I am "out there". They are essential to any and all "mission" that I do with Jesus. Do you tend to be on the "front lines" or are you more of a support person for someone who is. Do you feel God over you saying, "well done'? If so, enjoy His pleasure. If not, talk to God about this. What does He want from you? Remember many times He just wants us to be His and be enjoyed by Him. That is why it is so important to be able to sense *His* leading.

CHAPTER 23

Nothing is Beyond His Healing

April 18, 2014 – Robbed

Everything was going so well. We were just back from a wonderful vacation, getting the house unpacked, laundry done, groceries bought. Then, while I was getting the groceries out of the car, I was attacked and robbed right in front of my own house. It was dark outside, and though I saw someone running toward me out of the corner of my eye, I just assumed it was my oldest daughter playing a game on me. "Allie! That was too rough!" I yelled as my face slammed into the car frame. It wasn't until I felt someone pulling at the brand new, canvas purse around my neck that I realized I was under attack and being robbed.

All of a sudden, life changes. Watching the pictures and telling joy stories from our vacation turned into two hours of phone calls cancelling bank cards and an hour with the police. Then today, I was four hours at the police station, an hour looking for my purse in nearby dumpsters, two hours at the doctor's office looking over the burns on my neck, time processing with the kids what happened, and now time for me to process what happened.

Part of me just wants to act like it didn't happen and continue on with life as planned. But it *did* happen and plans have to change. So, not only am I struggling to deal with the fact that I was physically attacked, but I also have to accept that my time has been robbed from me as well.

I need to stop, to feel, to reflect, and to let Jesus meet me here. I find appreciation in the faces of my close friends who have called or come by to show me their support in the middle of this very traumatic event. I treasure each one of them.

"I want to be with You, Papa. I need to be with You. Tomorrow is Good Friday, and I am responsible for facilitating our house church meeting. I cannot possibly reflect on Your death with all of these emotions bouncing around in my mind, causing confusion, anger, and grief. I need to center myself and hear Your voice."

More appreciation memories come. I see myself looking at Allie, Anne, and Matty. I am enjoying them so much. I can see their golden hair and almost smell their soft fragrance. My lungs expand and I begin to calm.

Then I sense Jesus with me. He is enjoying me in the same way I enjoy my children. Another memory of sensing Him taking pleasure in me comes to mind. I remember being in Portugal watching the ocean hit up against the beautiful rocks. I felt God looking on, enjoying me as I was enjoying Him. I stay in this place of awe and wonder for a few minutes, enjoying His creation and my children.

"I feel that way about you, you know." I sense His thoughts unfold into mine.

"But, Lord, I would never let my children suffer if I could stop it," I throw back at Him. "You are supposed to be a loving Father! What kind of loving Father lets His children suffer? I just don't understand. We would never willingly stand by and watch someone attack our kids! Help me understand You! Why didn't You stop it?"

"I did stop it, Toni. That is what the cross was all about."

"But You did not stop it last night," I argue, trying to get my head around what He is saying. He obviously sees something I do not understand or see. I continue, "They could've done much worse to me, and You wouldn't have stopped that either. You did not stop the suffering. Your people suffer horrendous things at the hands of evil. The innocent suffer more than I can understand, much more than what happened to me last night. And yet You do nothing."

"Tomorrow is Good Friday," I add. "Yes, I know You died so that we could have eternal life, but I need to know what difference the cross makes in my life today. How does it make a difference in the pain that we live through?"

He is standing a few feet in front of me. He knows I am angry, yet He does not chide me. On the contrary, He begins to reveal Himself to me.

"Your heart and soul have been wounded, but they do not have to stay that way. Because I died, I can be with You right now, and I can heal you!" He says as He smiles. "I want to heal you. Come to Me, baby." He holds His arms outstretched, reaching for me.

Do I want to stay angry and hurt? Do I want to push Him out and blame Him for what has happened? Or do I want to accept what has happened to me and turn to Him for healing?

I run to Him and let Him hold me. He has healed me from so much pain over the years. I know He can make this pain go away, too.

"I know it hurts," He soothes as I weep in His arms. "I know it hurts when someone hurts you, especially when you don't deserve it." He pulls away just long enough to show me the nail scars in His hands. I rub my fingers along the marks He still bears.

"How do you heal me, Jesus?" I ask, tears still streaming.

"I have your heart safe inside of Me." He touches my chest where my heart lies. "They can hurt your body, but they can never take you away from Me. You are Mine! And because of the cross, I can be right here with you always."

"But where were You last night?" I sob, wanting to see with my own eyes where He was when the two men attacked. I know that if I can see Him there, then the memory will no longer cause pain.

I see an image of God the Father, the Son, and the Holy Spirit surrounding me outside, in the dark.

"I was all around you, surrounding you. He cannot take what is Mine. You are safely hidden in Me. Do not fear."

How can I not fear? We live in a world bathed in fear.

He continues, "I could stay relational on the cross because I did not fear what they were doing to Me." He smiles as if that were a pleasant memory of His.

"What do You mean, my Lord?" I ask, seeking clarification. I am not getting what He is saying.

"I did not fear what they were physically doing to me, because I knew that I would turn around and walk away from it whole. I need you to know to the core of your being, Toni, that nothing is beyond My healing. NOTHING, NOTHING, NOTHING is beyond My healing."

His words are so loud in my head that without realizing it I am screaming them out loud, "NOTHING, NOTHING, NOTHING is beyond My healing."

He takes my chin in his hand and raises my face so our eyes meet. "Do you believe Me?" He searches deep within my soul to see if I grasp what He is saying. "*Nothing* is beyond My healing – not torture, not rape, not child abuse, not murder, not sexual slavery, not mental illness. N*othing.*"

"But, all of these things hurt us so badly," I cry, feeling the pain of a world in suffering.

"Yes, they do physically hurt, but these evils are not to be feared, because they will all be healed. You will all walk away from this WHOLE because of what I did on the cross. This is the story I know that you do not yet see clearly. Because of the cross, I can comfort in the midst of the pain, I can emotionally heal any wound, and I will heal the body, as well, one day,"

This seems so crazy, but I can visually see the Kingdom of God coming. Souls are set free, bodies are healed for good, everything is made right. Everything is together again in the right amount, in the right time, in the right place, all is together. Shalom. I begin to cry again, but in awe of the healing that will be had. I can feel it in my bones.

"May Your healing come, my Lord, Jesus!" I bow to the floor in worship of One so great, and yet so tender. I touch the strap burns on my neck. The terrifying memory from last night has been replaced with an image of my Creator and Lover surrounding me and protecting my soul. I feel grateful and indebted that my Lord would meet me and take the time to explain Himself to me.

My fear has been replaced with passion and hope. Nothing is beyond His healing. I do not fear what man can do to me. Jesus' words in Matthew 10:28 vibrate within my body: "And do not fear those who kill the body but cannot kill the soul. Rather fear him who can destroy both soul and body in hell."

I am moved to beg God for healing today for humanity. "May Your Kingdom come! Use us to harvest the fields of shalom that are ripe in the world, and thrust more workers into the harvest."

CHAPTER 23

For Personal Reflection and Practice

1. What part of this story moved you the most?
2. Let God know how you felt reading the different happenings in this story. Ask His perspective on them.
3. What is it that He wants you to know regarding all of this?

CHAPTER 24

The Angry Eyes

June 23, 2014 – Trapped

Today was a terrible day. I was so tired that I slept all morning instead of doing any work. Maybe I'm fighting a virus or something. Allie had stayed home sick, as well. When I went to pick up the little ones from school, Allie had felt so bad that she had called the doctor on duty to come by the house to make sure she was okay.

I got the call from the emergency team while I was still at the school getting the other kids. "We think it is appendicitis. Would you like us to take her to the hospital in the ambulance, or would you like to take her yourself?"

I could not believe this was happening. Matt was out at San Geronimo leading a short-term mission team. I did not want to interrupt their activities. I knew I could probably find someone to watch the kids so that I could accompany Allie to the hospital.

I made a few calls from the school, secured a place for Matty and Annie to go for a few hours, and began the drive home to get Allie.

On my way home, I apparently almost cut someone off in traffic as I made a left-hand turn approaching our neighborhood. I had not seen the car coming. I only realized it when he pulled up close to my bumper. He had honked at me to let me know he had been forced to slow down because of my turn. It could *not* have been that bad, though, because he did not even have to slam on his breaks. All the same, I felt horrible. My mind, of course, had been on Allie at home alone with a possible case of appendicitis.

My heart rate sped up. I waved at the man behind me, trying to tell him I was sorry.

When I turned right into our neighborhood, the man behind me swerved around me and stopped right in front of me, pinching my car between his and the dumpster. I was trapped. The man proceeded to get out of his car. I could tell he was infuriated. I breathed deeply and said "Jesus help" out loud.

Realizing I had Matty and Annie in the car with me, I locked the doors and searched for my cell phone, thinking I would try to call the police.

The man approached my window screaming profanities at me in Spanish and began banging on my car window, demanding that I roll it down so that he could talk to me. He kept insulting me over and over again.

I looked into his eyes. They were filled with so much hate. I very respectfully said, "NO, I'm not going to roll down my window because you are being very disrespectful."

He got angrier, and I was afraid for my life. I honestly believe that if I had rolled down the window, that man would have killed me right there in front of my children. He continued to bang on the glass with such force that I prayed that God would keep it from breaking.

I breathed and tried to sense Jesus with me. "What do I do, Papa? How do I get out of this? Please help!"

The kids were asking questions, of course, and I managed to gently tell them that everything was going to be fine, that the man was very angry and that they needed to pray.

As I turned my attention back to the man, I finally caught some of the things he was saying about me.

"You are an idiot. You are an imbecile. You are a..." The list went on and on.

I heard countering words in my mind, "Toni, even if you had cut this man off in traffic, you still do not deserve to be treated this way. You are Mine. You are My beloved child!"

I immediately looked my attacker right in the eyes. We were nose-to-nose with an inch of glass between us, and I said, "No, I am not all those things you are saying. I am a beloved child of God."

As soon as the words left my lips, the man stopped instantly and backed away from the car with his hands up in the air as if I were holding him at gunpoint. He shook his head and ran away.

I could not believe it. I was so thankful and relieved that the attack had ended.

I arrived home, put the kids to play, and went to my bedroom to be alone and cry out the adrenaline that had just racked my body. I only had a few minutes, but in those five minutes, I did the "shalom for my body" exercises and called Matt to let him know what had just happened. I knew I needed to hear his voice. This gave me the joy and strength necessary to turn my attention to getting my daughter to the hospital. I would need to process more, but I had what I needed to be able to be present for my children right now.

June 24, 2014 – I was There

Here I am, Lord, coming for healing. In my mind, I am on the beach with You in the Isaiah 55 memory.

"What in the world happened to me on Monday?" I begin as You hold me close. "The kids were sick. I was a victim of road rage. I spent eight hours in the emergency room with Allie to find out that it was a pulled muscle and NOT appendicitis. And there is a short-term team here to boot! Where were You during the attack?"

"I was in the passenger seat right next to you, keeping you and the kids calm," as He begins, a smile comes across my face because I can see Him there. "I was inside of you keeping you calm for your kids. I was in the glass not breaking. And I was in your response, 'I am a child of God.'"

I can feel Him there in the memory inside of me, beside me, holding the window together. I am filled with gratitude and thankfulness. I am satisfied with how I responded, and I'm thankful that He gave me the right words to say to make the angry man leave.

Usually sensing Jesus with me in a traumatic memory is enough to bring complete healing to heart and mind. But for some reason, this offense is different. While I see Jesus there, I also see the man's angry face. And the angry face is closer to me and bigger than Jesus'. It is as if his angry eyes are etched in my physical brain. I cannot shake his glare. No matter where I look, no matter who I am looking at, I only see his eyes. This triggers fear in me. I don't want to drive anymore. I feel vulnerable and exposed and unprotected. I find myself looking for the angry man in cars on the street. I'm afraid I will see him again. Will You help me, please?

"This is war, Toni. You live on the front lines where My Kingdom is expanding into the darkness. You have a great platoon around you. Rest in them. Their eyes will replace that man's eyes in time. Let your people look at you in the eyes and see how precious you are to them, especially the men in your community: your dad, Diego, Jackson, Matt, and of course Me! The truth is that you are all vulnerable and weak. But know, My child, that you are not unprotected!"

My heart feels compassion for the man. I see him enslaved by his anger and probably deeply ashamed of the way he acted towards me. I wonder if he has ever yelled at his wife or his children the way he yelled at me. Do they know who he becomes when he is enraged? "Papa, I pray that You lead this man to you. I pray that he will learn how to still be himself even when he is angry. That he will learn to protect others from himself."

I am quieted. I am at peace. I will ask my friends in my community to look at me so that I can see their eyes enjoying me.

July 3, 2014 – Capacity for Suffering

Thank You, so much, Papa – Counselor, Healer. The last nine days have been a beautiful time of bonding with my community. One of my sweet friends said to me, "You feel weak, Toni, but it is not a weak person who says to someone attacking them, 'I am a beloved child of God!' I notice that you respond well when in moments of crisis like that, but then you fall apart afterward. There is a price to be paid when someone sins against us."

She was right. I pay the price in my own body and then my community pays a price, as well, as they help me pick up the pieces afterward.

Matt has been so understanding and tender. His eyes are slowly replacing the attackers. And then, on Friday during our house church meeting, my Uruguayan father sat and listened to me tell the entire story of the angry man. Even though I felt so awkward asking, he agreed to sit with me and look me in the eyes for a little while and enjoy me.

This was such a powerful, sweet time. He said that during those moments his soul completely shifted to seeing me as his daughter. I just cried feeling so loved that he would agree to be a part of God healing me.

I close my eyes and try to picture the rage in the eyes of the attacker. Thankfully, his eyes have been replaced by the eyes of my loving community. Thank You, Papa, for leading me into emotional healing. Thank you for taking what someone meant for harm and using it to bond our community together in such a beautiful way!

CHAPTER 24

For Personal Reflection and Practice

Dr. Wilder and our other mentors say that joy increases our capacity for suffering. Meaning that instead of being traumatized by bad things that happen, we can actually have the emotional strength to suffer well while staying relationally engaged and present.

Take Jesus for example. The Bible says, "For the joy that was set before him, He endured the cross," (Hebrews 12:2). This joy, this "being glad to be with the Father and with us," somehow enabled Him to suffer well what He went through. Even in the midst of His most difficult "traumatic" moments of being falsely accused, abandoned, and nailed to a tree, Jesus remained the same. He managed to care for His mother's future, encourage the thief who was dying next to Him, and forgive all who had been responsible for His death. He did not curse, hate, fear or lose hope.

More examples include the apostles. When they escaped from prison, Paul and Silas obeyed God and went right back to preaching in public. The reality that they could be killed at any moment did not faze them. Then, when they were flogged because of their public preaching, they left "rejoicing that they were counted worthy to suffer dishonor for the name" (Acts 5:41). They apparently were not traumatized by these events, but energized.

Then, we have the example of Stephen when the council members were enraged at him. He "full of the Holy Spirit, gazed into heaven and saw the glory of God, and Jesus standing at the right hand of God." In the midst of his excruciating execution, he was so elated with glory and joy that he called out, "Lord Jesus, receive my spirit!" and "do not hold this sin against them" (from Acts 7:55-60).

These examples go on and on throughout the New Testament and continue in Fox's Book of Martyrs. I believe God wants to train us to suffer well. Do you want to know God that closely?

1. What are your reactions to this story?

2. Have you suffered something similar or worse and have *not* been able to process it with someone yet? What I find so interesting in this story is that God did not just heal me completely by Himself. He directed me to go to my community for healing. Sometimes He wants to involve others in our healing process. Do you sense that you might have some traumatic experiences that need healing? I highly recommend finding a good counselor who is trained in Theophostic Prayer, the Immanuel Approach, or CRM: Comprehensive Resource Model.

3. Quiet yourself, go to an interactive appreciation memory, ask God what you need to know regarding the trauma in your life.

PART VI

· · · · ·

*A New Chapter
(2014-2015)*

Becoming a Vibrant Family of Jesus

January 25, 2014 – Learning to Lead

I met John White a few weeks back on a Life Model Works Google hangout. He demonstrated leadership skills that blew me away. He managed to create a sense of belonging among 15 total strangers and gently support the facilitator of the meeting in implementing a structure that enabled us to make decisions and move forward on a project, all within 45 minutes. I was impressed.

I want to learn to navigate group discussions the way he does. I want to learn how to listen and engage others in a non-threatening way. We seem to speak the same language in so many different areas and yet, I sense he is farther along than we are on the maturity path, as well as the church planting path.

So, I wrote him immediately, and a week later, he agreed to mentor Matt and me. We are so thankful for an elder and church planting mentor coming into our lives at this time. We have sensed intuitively how the church will look and spread here in Uruguay, but we have not been able to articulate or reproduce what we see.

John shared with us the foundations of Luke 10, the Church Planting Community of Practice he co-founded (www.lk10.com). Their vision is to fulfill the Great Commission by seeing a "vibrant family of Jesus" (small groups, house church, etc.) within easy reach of every person, in every region and people group on earth. They plan to do this by connecting and equipping emerging house church leaders around the world.

Our conversation last week and subsequent training has been so enlightening and course altering that I must get it out on paper.

He asked us, "What would it take to see a vibrant family of Jesus within easy reach of every person on the planet?"

Having earned a Master's Degree in Church Planting, it is a question Matt and I have been pondering for a long time now, with the best thinkers on the subject. And yet, we have not been satisfied with what we have found thus far.

Matt and I began to reflect with John about our church experiences, our families of origin, and why we felt so strongly about getting faith out of the church building and into our homes.

My earliest memories of going to traditional church bring a smile to my face and warmth to my heart. VBS, Vacation Bible School, was my favorite summer activity. Because both of my parents worked full time, they were more than happy to enroll me in every church that offered free care. I can still remember the excitement over snack time where I would feel comforted by the juice and cookies and so wanted by the smiles on the faces around me. The music, the puppets, the Bible stories were all part of the emotion, as well. I longed for those times where I, thankfully, consistently experienced safety, warmth, and love. I felt emotionally and spiritually nurtured, which was something I longed for in my own family.

When I was 8 years old, unbeknownst to me, my parents were on the brink of divorce and needed help. Thankfully, they had found some refuge in a church that offered free marital counseling and, as a result, our family began to attend regularly. I laugh as I think of running around the halls of our enormous church building playing hide and seek with the other kids and sneaking ice out of the ice machine. We felt like we owned the building; we were at home there. There was a sense of belonging that contained us as children. All of us came from different backgrounds, but we were all looking for the same things: safety, connection, belonging, joy. And we found them there, inside the church building.

By the time I was 14, however, I longed for something more. I wanted the safety, connection, belonging, and joy that I sensed inside the church to move out of that building and into my own home and school where I lived my daily life. I began wondering why seven years of being actively involved in church had not helped us as a family *be* church together. We knew more about the Bible, what it expected from us, what we *should* do and how we *should* be, but it seemed like there was a disconnect of some sort, because it did not seem to affect the way we related to each other. We still felt spiritually and emotionally disconnected as a family.

I also wondered why so many of my friends all said they believed in God and went to church, and yet our life at school was void of any spiritual connection. Instead, it was filled with out-of-control gossip, hate, conflict, depression, sex, betrayal, and alcohol.

I felt frustrated and angry. "Why wasn't Christ making a difference in my daily life?" was the question haunting me. "If God is the God of the Bible," I thought, "then surely He came to make a difference in my *real* life, not just in my church life. How do I get my faith out of the building and into my daily life, out of my personal quiet time and into the relationships around me? How do I bring it home?"

The feeling was like having something powerful, like a train, and yet lacking the tracks to move it on. What good is a train without the track? I could make my home there, find comfort and shelter there, but I could not get anywhere I wanted to go, nor offer this hope to others. My train was only so big.

It was around this time that Matt and I met. Never having

attended church regularly, he had come to Christ at 16 in a somewhat desperate search to make sense of all of the pain in his life. Divorced parents, sex, drugs, and porn surrounding him, he found solace in the quietness of Christ. In the institutional church, he found some sort of structure to calm the chaos.

We happened into each other's lives and, determined to see Christ made real in the real world, embarked on a journey together, leaving our trains behind in search of materials to build some sort of train track, some way of connecting the world outside of the church to the amazing Christ-hope the church has to offer.

We knew small groups were more effective in creating real life change. During our seminary studies, we focused on cell church planting, which emphasized a small group structure. However, after 16 years of church planting in Uruguay, this model was still not working. In fact, no model had yet become truly effective and reproducible. Most Uruguayans work 70-hour work weeks, never see their children, and have no church culture whatsoever. The type of church they need has to be able to function within the family system, not only outside of it.

In all of our time there, we had managed to nurture an emotionally healthy family system of 30 or so. But again, it felt like we had built a train, yet were still lacking the tracks to move it on.

After sharing all of this with John, he asked another question, "How small can it be and still be a church?"

Matt was smart and quick. "Two. You know, Matthew 18:20: 'For where two or three are gathered in my name, there am I among them...' That thing."

Like a well-trained coach, John continued the questions, "And what would have to happen in order for it to be considered a 'church'?"

We both thought about the Great Commandment and the Great Commission. And I replied, "You'd have to love God and love each other, and make disciples. Our mission, Comunitas International, says it this way, communion with God, community with each other and life-giving mission together."

"And how often would they meet?" His questions seemed so basic, so simple. We have thought this through a thousand times. But we had no idea where he was going, so we played along.

Verses came to mind and we summarized, "Encourage each other daily, as long as it is called today" (Hebrews 3:13, NIV). "They met together daily" (Acts 2:46).

Our minds were churning. Our little community of 30 could never meet together daily. While we do life together in every way possible, we still only see everybody two or three times a week at most. Each one has their own family to take care of.

The only person I see daily is Matt and maybe my best friend who is like a sister here.

At this realization, it slowly started to hit us with real force. "That's... what... Matt... and... I... are...." I think out loud. "We are two people who gather in Jesus' name, we commune with God together, we enjoy community together, and we are on mission."

And then, the reality sinks in: we are not only *starting* a church plant, our FAMILY already *IS* a church plant, and we are currently nurturing the seedlings of four other churches. Why have we never thought that a family unit is a valid form of church?

Then, the clinching question came: **"Have you truly embraced the fact that you two and your children *are* a church?"**

"No." The answer was shocking to me and enlightening at the same time. For years now, I have wondered how to provide a safe space for my own children to explore the claims of Christ as a family. Traditional "family devotions" never worked with our kids or us. I just sought to live so closely to Jesus that they could smell Him on me! Launching Godly Play at the local international English-speaking church was my way as a mother of creating a Christian education space for my children. While it is an amazing space, again, I wanted to know how could I bring it home, out of the church building and into my family?

John's questions continued, "What could two people do to BE church with each other? What rhythms and practices could they, and any other family, do, that would have them follow Jesus' leadership to 'love God, love each other, and make disciples'?"

That was the question my heart had been pondering my entire life. I was ready for the answer!

John suggested two basic and simple practices: "Checking-in" and "listening." Matt and I were amazed to see how these practices were identical to some of our relational-skill exercises from our Thrive training. We had just never thought about doing them together and embracing them as the "practices of the church." But as John shared, it made so much sense!

Checking-in means taking a few minutes to share with each other how we are feeling, without needing to fix, change, or invalidate each other. In my Thrive language, this was practicing joy together, being glad to be together no matter what! While so simple, offering a listening ear to each other is incredibly difficult at times!

Then, "listening" refers to taking a few minutes of silence to practice sensing how God feels about being with us, and what we need to know as a couple or family. After these minutes of silence, we share with each other and seek to "pay attention" to what God might be saying to us. Maybe He wants us to ponder His stories from His Word. Maybe He wants us to cook for our sick neighbor. Maybe He wants us to do something fun as a family to build our joy. Again, Thrive would call this developing the skill of "God sight" or "Immanuel Lifestyle."

John closed our time together that day challenging us to begin these practices as close to daily as possible. He sent us his 4-week course, and after a time of "listening" to God together, he shared, "Matt and Toni, I sense that God will use you to start a church planting movement in Uruguay that will change that nation. And it will actually just flow from you. It will not even feel like work, it will be that easy."

We began the course immediately, and for the first time in

years, Matt has become excited about being in Jesus' presence with the kids and me! I see a renewed passion for church planting take over his heart that had grown weary and discouraged over the lack of movement all these years.

Now we have a track to move our train on with two solid rails: "checking-in" and "listening." I am so encouraged because these two practices embody everything we have learned from Thrive about relational skills and maturity. If two people practice these two rhythms as close to daily as possible, they grow their ability to experience joy, to soothe themselves, to bond with each other, and quiet together. They will create moments of appreciation, be able to see their heart values, begin to sense when they overwhelm each other. They will learn to see what God sees and be able to return to joy from all of their difficult emotions. And, as they invite their children and/or friends into this space, family bonds and healthy, transformative, joy-filled community emerges.

I am amazed at how these two practices answer the question, "What does it really *look* like to love one another, love God, and make disciples?" I can see that as God brings people to us, and we teach them to practice these simple, but challenging rhythms, they will come to value their homes/families as churches. They will own the responsibility of leading their families well, relationally and spiritually. Church planting could now become a movement by praying for God to bring us "workers for the harvest" (Luke 10:2) and then by training and coaching these pairs!

The hope regarding church planting here in Uruguay is something I never dreamed would come. We can see parents as pastors, houses as churches, and church buildings as training centers. What if every Christian couple we knew were practicing these rhythms and inviting others into this God-space with them? It very well could start a revolution! May it be so, in Your timing, Papa, God.

CHAPTER 25

For Personal Reflection and Practice

When we discovered LK 10, the interesting thing for Matt and I was that none of these concepts were new to us, in and of themselves. We were great at sharing our emotions. We also had been working on "listening" to Jesus for years. We had just never tried to do these things as "rhythms of church." It was as if these practices, which are normally learned in counseling situations, were being repurposed for daily use!

In other words, it was not so much the actual exercises that were new to us. What was new was the idea that these rhythms could be the foundational rhythms for being church together, and, that our family of five is a valid expression of church in this world. This freed us to *value* our family and actually give them the time it takes to pastorally care for those inside of our home. Many Pastors and Missionaries unfortunately often feel guilty for caring well for their little ones.

1. Do you see your family as a valid expression of the church? Do you value serving them and creating spiritual space for them as important as teaching a Sunday School class or leading a programed ministry? Not that I am suggesting either/or, but many people I know "leave" their family in order to participate in Church leadership. Since volunteering at church gets validation of your commitment to Christ, some people actually serve at church at the expense of their family! What if churches trained parents to give Pastoral Care to their own families and saw every family as a mini-church within that congregation?

2. Can you imagine a church where every single couple was

checking-in with each other and listening to Jesus as close to every day as possible, and leading their family to do the same? What would it look like? How would that church be different than others?

3. How would your family be different if you, and one other person in your home, were checking-in and listening with each other as close to daily as possible? What would hinder you from taking that next step? What would hinder others in your family from joining in? What resources do you feel like you would need in order to begin something so radical?

It is incredible that something so "simple," as sharing our emotions and practicing "sensing" God's presence with us, can be so incredibly hard for people to do together. Attempting to live at this level of intimacy will immediately reveal the lack of trust and/or relational depth that exists in the relationship/community/family. We simply cannot go this deep with people we do not trust, or with groups that are not "safe" emotionally for us.

My larger family is only now developing the trust and intimacy necessary to even consider trying to practice these rhythms together. While I have wanted this level of relationship for years, I have had to trust the process and work on becoming a safe person for those in my family. I have had to be willing to listen to how I impact them, how my pride has affected them over the years, and what I need to work on in order for them to feel safe with me. It has seemed like a long process, but real intimacy and health cannot be rushed. To try to rush others is a complete disrespect of their emotional process. We cannot force others to trust us or enjoy us. We can only control our own actions, attitudes, and responses. We can enjoy, love, and invite.

If you would like to pursue training in how to become a "vibrant family of Jesus" contact Lk10 at www.lk10.com.

CHAPTER 26

Taking Ground

May 10, 2014 – No Longer Under Siege

Last night, we were praying with some retiring, veteran
missionaries, Tom and Tina, at our dining room table in
Montevideo. It would be our last time to sit together in person
asking Jesus for Uruguay before they began the next season of
their life. Practicing the rhythms of church that now seem second
nature to us, we went around the table doing a "check-in,"
followed by a time of listening to Jesus for Uruguay.

"Lord, is there anything You want us to know about what
You are doing here?" we asked. Then we sat in silence, paying
attention to the subtleties and nuances of the impressions in our
own souls. We tried to listen and discern for the "still, small
voice" that spoke to Elijah in the cave. We noticed sensations,
images, feelings, or thoughts that spontaneously popped into our
minds.

During the quiet, I had a picture of all of the missionaries,
pastors, and Christian workers in Uruguay under a big, transparent
dome that was pressing in on us. It sought to crush us and take the

small bit of ground we were occupying.

At the same time, God's Spirit was there with us, holding enemy forces at bay, while we fought to bring joy, health, and hope to those we could reach. Supplies dwindled, needs increased. Scarcity hit like the kind that comes when you are under siege.

And then the unthinkable happened. All of a sudden, the dome shook and then burst outward into the darkness beyond. We stood amazed at the power of God! Then I sensed the words, "Now go, take back the ground the enemy has stolen from you, in your own hearts, in your families, in your communities, your schools, your businesses, and in the entire culture!"

I sensed God saying that the Christians in Uruguay have been under siege and holding ground for the last 20 or so years. But now, the time is shifting, and it is time to take back ground for the Kingdom in every area of society.

We sat together in awe as each one shared their impressions of what God was doing in our midst. By the end of the night, it was very clear that a monumental spiritual shift was on the horizon for the nation of Uruguay, and our hearts long to be a part of it!

August 15, 2014 – Continue Following Me

Almost every day I come to You and confess that we do not have the resources necessary to continue on here in Uruguay, and yet there are more and more opportunities for conferences and leadership training. We are moving forward with the Geronimo Center for Innovation and Leadership and are seeing incredible results in the schools and businesses we have been invited into.

I am convinced that God wants to use this Center to launch a church planting movement in Uruguay that not only assures that there is a joy-filled, vibrant family of Jesus within reach of every person, but also creates a revolution of hope and joy that specifically addresses the issues of mental illness and depression in that country. It is such an exciting time to be here!

However, we are suffering. Financially, we are suffering from being underfunded for so long, adding two more children, living through the economic crisis of 2008, purchasing the retreat center, and starting a missional business.

It seems that our family's emotional health is in distress, as well. Matt has taken some extremely hard hits these last few years. After pushing hard to raise the funds for the retreat center, he dove right into starting the business. While he made headway in Uruguay like no one ever dreamed possible, the stress has taken its toll. He is dangerously tired.

Then there is our oldest daughter. She has always wanted to live in the States and, while she has made it the best she can here, Uruguay has been hostile to her soul. No matter how much we as a family do to create joy, she is not in a joyful environment outside of us. She needs more than we can give. She is struggling like never before, and I know she needs professional help we can only get in the States.

"What are we to do, Papa? How can I leave Uruguay right now when we are finally seeing fruit from our seventeen years of work here, when the tide is changing and movement is finally happening?!"

I sense You on the beach. I am pacing in front of You. I do *not* want to hear what You might have to say to me. I do *not* want to leave. It cannot possibly be Your will.

"Toni," You begin as You watch me pace, "in order to take ground, you need to re-source and resupply. No one ever begins an attack under-resourced. It is the nature of a siege to live without. But the siege is over. It is time to prepare for what is next. I want to recover and restore for you all that has been lost during the siege. You are not the only ones who will be regrouping in order to reengage. I am removing many of the missionaries who need to rest for a season."

His perspective sounds inviting. I stop pacing and face Him. "We are due for a three-month furlough in December. Is that what

You're talking about?"

"You are not ready to hear what I have to say about that." He smiles compassionately. "Just continue following Me. I will show you the way."

CHAPTER 26

For Personal Reflection and Practice

1. As you read this chapter what did you feel?

2. I firmly believe that God is seeking people to join us on this amazing mission of "launching a church planting movement in Uruguay that not only assures that there is a joy-filled, vibrant family of Jesus within reach of every person, but also creates a revolution of hope and joy that specifically addresses the issues of mental illness and depression in that country." I also believe that God is not restricted to Uruguay. I am sensing Him calling us to serve Globally with this Center. If your heart sped up as you read this mission, ask the Holy Spirit what He would like to say to you about this. Please do not hesitate to contact us if you would like to somehow be involved in bringing hope to the world in this way. For more information about the Geronimo Center or to become a partner, go to www.christianassociates.org/where/latin-america/geronimo-center.

3. I love the way Jesus is so gentle with me in the second story. He knew there was only so much I could handle. Is there something you are afraid He might say to you? Tell Him how you are feeling and ask Him to show you His perspective.

CHAPTER 27

Hope from Ashes

October 15, 2014 - Weak, Yet Strong

Yesterday at 11am, we received the call that my father-in-law had suffered a massive stroke and was gone. By 7pm, I had soothed myself, picked up the kids from school, taught a workshop, organized and executed a plan to leave our precious three children, and boarded a plane with my husband headed for the United States. We are shell shocked, but feel so held by our Lord.

For the last years, it has been absolutely mind-boggling how I can be in such emotionally distressing circumstances and yet feel so held by Jesus at the same time. It is a paradox, but a beautifully welcomed one.

I am now sitting on my third plane with Matt. Tears flow as I think about what my precious spouse is about to face. His father was his best friend and his greatest cheerleader. He was about to visit us again in Uruguay. He believed so passionately in San Geronimo and was eager to get back there to see all that had developed since the beginning.

I ask, "Papa, how will my husband get through this?"

I see a large hand underneath Matt making him strong, but also letting him be weak at the same time. I know I can trust him to God's care. I breathe, put my hand in his, and look into his eyes with the assuredness that he will get through.

October 17, 2014 – Be There

Today is the funeral. In the last two days I have seen my husband do some of the most amazing relational work in his life: quieting himself, listening to You, feeling You holding him, grieving but not getting lost there. Joy is holding onto him and sustaining him.

Every now and then, it hits me, the gravity of what has happened. We both were brought to tears when we heard the news that his dad wants his ashes to be buried at San Geronimo and, instead of flowers, he requested people to donate funds to the Center.

We listened to You, Papa, yesterday about what You wanted the memorial service to be like. We sensed that it can be a joy-filled, hope-filled time to communally remember, celebrate, and grieve.

"Is there anything You want me to know today, Papa?"

"Be there for Matt. Don't leave his side. You are strength and joy to him right now. He is the only one who matters to you today. Do not leave him to be there for someone else. Keep your eyes on him."

I cry as I hear this. "Thank You for permission to love my husband, to see him as important, and to honor him today. Thank You, Papa."

October 25, 2014 – Making Room to Grieve

Life as we know it is too much to bear. We landed in Uruguay today, and as I looked out onto the city, a wave of grief washed over me. My soul immediately pushed it away. I grabbed Matt's hand, and fully aware of the lack of physical and emotional safety we were returning to, stated the obvious: "There is no way we can grieve while we are in Uruguay. We will need people to care for our children at times so that we can get away. We will need to be held by a community, instead of holding a community together."

We have known for years that we are not yet at an elder stage of maturity, where we are free to sacrificially care for an entire community. We still have little children that need much of our resources.

At the beginning of this year, we re-structured our larger community by families so that we were only responsible for our little church in our home. That freed us to train other "parents (and singles) as pastors," those of us who see our homes as churches. These weekly meetings have served to practice our rhythms together, giving us guidance as a larger body, and supporting the development of the necessary skills we all need to pastor well.

The reality is, however, that there are no elders for Matt and me here. We have been Skyping for over a year now with mentors and counselors to try to meet these needs that we have, but it has barely sustained us.

Then, when we arrived home from the funeral, suitcases still packed, our oldest daughter completely tanked.

"I am so lonely here and isolated! I need to go home to live in the States. I have no friends here, and I am failing school, and I am depressed. You brought me to the most depressive nation in all of the Americas, and you expect me to be happy? To thrive?"

My heart was broken for her.

"Why is the way so unclear to me, Papa?" I come for guidance.

"Because you don't want to see it, My child." I sense His gentle words. Tears begin to flow.

"What do I need to know about my daughter?" I beg Him, ready to see whatever is necessary.

"Do not emotionally abandon her. Meet her where she is. You

MUST care for your weak, just like I care for you. You MUST go at her pace. It is NOT My will that you move forward in mission and leave the wounded behind! She IS your church!"

I see images of when she was younger, when I did not know how to meet her emotional needs, moments I deeply regret.

"You have another chance now," I sense Papa saying. "It is not too late."

Hope breaks into my grief. Oh, how I have needed Papa's words today. The maturing He is asking me to do feels like it will mean sacrificing my entire life's work. And, yet, it feels so right to do so. I feel like Abraham having to sacrifice Isaac, except my Isaac is our mission here in Uruguay.

I crumble to the floor. I don't know if I have the strength to do it. I am also afraid for the little ones. They have finally adjusted to living in Uruguay. They LOVE it here. What will happen to them? I think my heart will be torn in two.

"I don't think I have the emotional strength right now to pack my house and organize all the details for an international move. Oh, God, just cooking everyday here and cleaning is overwhelming. No fast food, no paper plates, everything has to be made from scratch. What do I need to know to get me through this?" I cry out of the brokenness of my heart.

"You are entering a new season of life, My daughter. It has been a beautiful five years in this home, raising your babies. But it is time to move on."

He pauses because He knows I need time to feel the weight of what He is saying to me. I double over in pain as if someone is physically ripping my stomach out. The pit in my stomach is there. He holds me as I cry. I know how badly I am hurting, but I can also sense hope. I am not lost in hopeless despair; I am only grieving and feeling the very real pain of loss.

As I quiet, He continues, "I have beautiful surprises for you while you are in the States. Remember the time of mourning will end, and the time of celebration will come. Remember, the time of holding ground is over, and the time of taking back ground has begun. Give yourself to the process, and I will be the wind in your sails. Relax, rest, and let Me carry you."

Memories of Matty's birth five years ago come to mind and a new wave of pain rolls over me. I ask, "Do I need to know something about what happened then?"

"You are still mourning Matty's premature birth and all that was lost during those three months. Life as you knew it ceased, never to be the same again. He is your gift, but he came at a great loss, at a great price to all in your family and your community. He is worth your very life. But you still need to grieve all that was lost to you."

I feel validated and seen. It is okay to mourn. Then Anne comes to mind, and I am so scared for her. She hates change and has worked so hard to belong here.

He speaks before I can even ask the questions. "I have your Anne," He says with an enormous smile on His face. "See the joy in her?"

"Yes, Papa, but it is so fragile. She hates change. She hates new schools. She is so introverted. Will she be okay through all of this?"

"Yes, My sweet baby. She will be fine."

"How will I ever get her back here?" I wonder. "It's like her soul is ripped apart every time we go and come."

"Leave that to Me. You are pulling out now to come back stronger. Remember, no army tries to do battle without the resources they need. You are NOT on the defensive anymore. You are attacking the enemy's territory, and you will need all the resources to do so. I will give them to you. Trust Me and follow."

"Yes, my Lord. Thank You."

"Cry no more over this. See the future and believe!"

I see my oldest in a life-giving relationship with Jesus Himself. I see Matt, old and gray, dancing in the fields of San Geronimo, celebrating all that God has done. I see myself, old and gray, standing on the porch with a cup of coffee in my hand. I am filled with deep satisfaction as I watch my husband dance before our Lord and Creator. I know that God has been faithful and that we have followed. All is in the right place, in the right time, in the right amount. I see shalom.

I walk away filled with peace and hope, ready to follow Him wherever He leads. I know how the story ends, for I have the images etched into my soul. They are as real as memories I have lived. It is like they are memories of the future. I do not understand how this can be, but I think for the first time in my life, I fully grasp what the Hebrews writer meant when he said, "Now faith is the assurance of things hoped for, the conviction of things not seen" (11:1).

CHAPTER 27

For Personal Reflection and Practice

It is amazing to me how we can call out faith in others when we are centered in Christ's presence ourselves. Had I looked at Matt with fear in my eyes that moment on the plane, he might have crumbled. I would have transmitted to him my anxiety. But, as I stilled my fear in Jesus' presence and saw His reality, I was able to instill confidence and peace in Matt that he was going to be okay. I was glad to be with him no matter what. Life Model Works calls this "joy strength." We actually draw strength from each other when we are glad to be together no matter what is happening to us. Unfortunately, there have been times when I sewed doubt and fear into those around me because I did not take the time to still myself and listen first before interacting.

1. Ask yourself if there is a situation that you are facing that is causing you anxiety.

2. Breathe deeply a few times and scan your body. How are you feeling physically?

3. Close your eyes and go to an appreciation memory (as described previously in this book).

4. Ask Jesus how He feels about being with you.

5. Ask Jesus where He was in that appreciation memory.

6. Pay attention to thoughts, words, images, impressions, physical sensations, etc.

7. If you sense Him, receive from Him.

8. Share with Him all you are feeling regarding the situation at hand.

9. Ask Him what you need to know in order to get through what you are facing.

10. Is there someone who can be glad with you in this situation? Ask God to show you who you can share with that will amplify your "joy strength" (and vice versa).

A Few of the Gifts

December 21, 2014 – My Family of Origin

We have done it. We have moved. We will spend the next two weeks at my parents' house to rest and enjoy Christmas before we branch out on our own.

I had a wonderful time with my sister yesterday! Mom arranged everything so that we could go shopping together. I had no idea we would end up hanging out for hours! She asked me about our decision to come Stateside. "So, what happened when you got back to Uruguay after the funeral? You had said, 'All hell broke loose!' What did you mean by that?"

I felt loved by her that she would want to know what I had been going through. It felt like a gift of water to a thirsty soul. I briefly shared what had happened to move us to decide to take this sabbatical. I could see that she was fully aware of how hard the last few weeks had been on me. She leaned in to hold me. I cried, releasing some of the sadness. As she continued holding me, I felt loved, safe, and connected.

This is such a gift, Papa. I am excited about the opportunity to have true heart-to-heart connection with my birth family. It is a dream come true.

January 29, 2015 – My Nannie

My grandmother was taken in for emergency surgery this morning. They say she might have air in her blood. Thank You, Papa that we were just with her a few weeks ago. Please be gracious and merciful to us. Help us sense You and walk with You through this.

Last night for some reason, at bedtime, I was overwhelmed with gratitude for my little babies. In the midst of being so thankful, grief came over me as I mourned losing those three months with my Anne because of Matty's premature birth. His early coming affected our relationship with both her and Allie. They both were in major transition with having just left the States, moving into a new home, and beginning a new school.

It felt good to mourn and be in touch with all that was lost. I just sat in Your arms and cried. Thank You for being there for me and helping me feel.

January 30, 2015 – Family Retreat

Today, I spent the day at the hospital with Nannie and the entire family. It is so precious to see all of my cousins all grown up and overcoming the obstacles life has thrown at them. I have not seen them in some years. And while I am so sad our Nannie is in the hospital, this week has been like a retreat with the whole family. I am enjoying them so much. Thank You for this gift.

February 2, 2015 – Yours

We are on day five of 24-7 care for Nannie in ICU. Thankfully, I got a good sleep last night! It was so needed. There are just three of us who can take shifts to be with her. I am so thankful that I get to be here to do this.

I feel strange today. 1 Thessalonians 4:17 is going through my head: "Then we who are alive and remain will be caught up with those in the clouds, to meet the Lord in the air" (NASB). I am shaking slightly, adrenaline probably. I feel as though the end of my grandmother's life is near. I don't feel strong at all. I feel so weak.

"Papa, what do You want me to know today?"

I see the image of my Nannie happily swinging in His arms. He has picked her up, snuggled her into His chest, and is enjoying her like never before.

"Is that how this ends?" I sense His affirmation.

"How does it end for us, though? Help me, Papa, attune with those around me today. Please help me see them. Let my hands and mouth and eyes be Yours."

January 4, 2015 – You are with Us

My grandmother, Nannie, breathed her last breath early this morning, surrounded by her loved ones encouraging her to run into the arms of Jesus. It was such an amazing and beautiful moment that the nurse came to me seconds afterward and said, "I have never seen a family sense the presence of Jesus so strongly when a loved one was dying. That was indeed a gift to me. I usually ask if you need a pastor, but I see you have Jesus Himself with you!"

It was a holy moment I will never forget, and a gift I will carry with me throughout my years. My Nannie was the bedrock of our family and it would have been unbearable to have missed her home-going and the chance to remember and mourn with my family.

Thank You, God, that You would have me here for this time. When You said You had good gifts for me in the States, I never dreamed this would be one. Thank You so much.

June 18, 2015 – The Mountains and Memories

Last week, I was on the tram between Gatlinburg and Ober Gatlinburg with my children, my husband, and my parents. I was having flashbacks of being 7 years old, the current age of my youngest daughter, riding that same tram. A huge smile came across my face as I realized that the last time I had seen those mountains, I was with my parents 34 years ago! As I looked out at the blanket of rolling peaks before me, tears welled up in my eyes, and a fullness swelled in my chest. I could feel it all the way up to my throat. I was in awe and wonder. How could something be so beautiful? So vast?

I was also filled with gratitude that God would allow me to return here with my parents AND my own children. For ten years now, we have been wanting to make this trip together, and now, it was finally happening.

Where was Jesus, I wondered. I saw His face imposed over the mountains. This seemed silly to me, so I engaged playfully, "What are You trying to say to me?"

As I sensed the vastness and greatness of all of the enormous peaks and ridges around me, I could hear Him say, "I am bigger than even these. And I am enveloping you in My presence, just like they are doing."

I took a deep breath and looked deeply at my personal people who were with me in the tram.

"How do You feel about being with me?" I continued with Jesus.

All of a sudden, in my mind's eye, I could see monkeys

scampering along the tramway about to attack the tramcar. I looked to the mountains to see God's face, but realized that He had become the tramcar itself. He felt protective of me. He was protecting me. He wanted me to know that He is jealous for me, and that I am surrounded by Him.

Tears came to my eyes right there in the tramcar. I didn't expect this. I didn't even know I was feeling unprotected. But as I received these images, my entire mood shifted, like a weight I did not even know I was carrying had been removed.

The last three months have been incredibly difficult. We have faced problems in our family that I thought would take me down. But He wants me to know He is protecting me. I am His. I can accept the things that are happening around me, and I can surrender to His way.

I thank You, Papa, for all of the professional help You are providing for us. We have had the best social workers, counselors, and coaches around us helping us understand the transitions we are going through.

We have decided to stay for at least three more years to see our oldest through high school. That is one of the hardest decisions I have ever had to make. I cannot explain how complex this feels in my soul. I hold on to all the images You have given me, and I try to rest.

CHAPTER 28

For Personal Reflection and Practice

What is your understanding of grief? How do you feel about mourning or grieving, not just the loss of a loved one, but also the loss of hopes, dreams, expectations, desires?

For me, grief was hard to recognize at first. Many times it comes with wonderful joy as well, making it hard to give myself permission to grieve. For example, when Matty was born prematurely, we lost three months of "normal" life with our other two children. Yet, there was so much to be thankful for, that it was hard to give myself permission to grieve. It was like I felt guilty or unappreciative if I focused on what I had lost. But, thankfully, God Himself gave me permission to grieve. He showed me that I was not being ungrateful for feeling the losses that had occurred.

As I have learned to recognize it in myself, I have been able to give myself permission to be sad and mourn the losses I feel. Otherwise I end up trying to numb them without even realizing it, another cup of coffee, another glass of wine, a shopping spree, a chocolate brownie, launch another ministry, share the gospel with one more person. Our pain numbing activities have no end and only lead to isolation and depression. The only healthy way forward is through it with the presence of our Creator and/or others who are glad to be with us no matter what.

1. Go to an interactive appreciation memory if you have one.

2. Ask yourself and God if there is anything you are sad about losing.

3. Listen. Journal everything that comes to mind.

4. Ask Jesus what He thinks about all of that and what you need to know.

5. Share with someone else what you experienced.

PART VII

· · · · ·

The Chrysalis
(2015)

"I feel like I have been inside a chrysalis the last few months. Due to issues with my children and my husband, I have felt pressed in on like never before. As I have struggled against these pressures, wounded areas of my soul have become exposed. These are areas I have sensed present with me throughout my life, but yet, could never understand nor heal. The following is my struggle to break free and finally fly."

2015, November

It's that Time of Year

October 2007

It is that time of year again
When echoes call out to me.
They reach out from my past
Grasping to lay hold of my heart.

Why are they still present within?
What keeps them there lying dormant
Like seeds until the spring comes
and calls them forth into bloom?

Layers and layers of pain
Trying to sort themselves out.
Lies that were once true
Trying to convince me they are still right.

Come forth and show yourselves,
You demons from the past.
Come into the light and release your pain
Into the presence of a new reality,
That you might know the truth
And that it might set you free.

For the Joy Set Before Me

September 3, 2015 – Soul Space

More loss to mourn. Sometimes I think I will never stop crying. So much crying. This whole week has been consumed with the job decision. Can I handle Matt working full time right now while we are on sabbatical? Can I stand in what I know to be true, even if he is denying that very truth?

We have experienced several years of deep intimacy and joy between us. He has been present like never before in our marriage and in our community. Life has been more difficult than ever, but we have stayed well connected to each other and to Jesus through it all.

But he is not himself. The last three weeks have been so difficult. He is shut down again. Yesterday morning, he said to me, "Toni, I am asking that you die to your dreams, your desires, and your needs so that I can go to work half-time for 5 weeks and then full time after that."

I was shell-shocked. To me it looks like he is running from his pain. He is taking a job to hide the hurt and not have to do the work of sabbatical. He is stealing my time, as well, and taking my sabbatical away from me. How will he heal if he is running from the process and shutting himself down to me relationally?

The hole he ripped through me by asking me to sacrifice was unbearable. I have a right to heal and to rest. He is asking me to give that up so he can numb and run? I know it does not look that way to him. Who will protect me? Who will defend me?

I was so angry at Matt for asking that of me, that it did not even occur to me to simply say, "NO. Let's find another solution." I was lost in emotion, unable to negotiate for my needs to be met. The only thing I could do was run, try to get safe, be with someone who would protect me.

What is this pain about? I ball up and put my hands and arms over my head to protect myself. Anger, sadness, grief, injustice all come like waves through my body as I rock, trying to calm the storm.

I drive to a friend's house. Safe. Not alone. I find a refuge where I could find my Refuge.

I get so tripped up by needing Matt to care for me. I want him to stop what he is doing because he sees how much it is hurting me. But when it seems like he is NOT doing that, I go into a whirlwind of pity, grief, anger, and sadness. I call my mentor for help.

He asks me, "How did Jesus endure the cross?"

I think. Surely I know this answer, but I am so trapped in pain, it is impossible to access.

"For the joy set before Him. Remember? The thought of being together with you, me, and God gave Him so much 'joy strength' that it motivated Him to endure the ultimate of suffering. So, ask Him, what is the joy set before you?"

In the safety of my mentor's presence, I quiet myself by breathing deeply and seeking an interactive appreciation memory. I ask my Lord, "What is the joy set before me?"

Jesus leads me through the Isaiah experience that we had together years ago. I can feel it present with me now. How He found me alone, thirsty, desperate, hungry, and hurt. How He offered me food, water, and joy. How He carried me for miles, for days, safe in His arms. How He sat me down at a table prepared just for me and Him, white table cloth, wine glasses, sand beneath our feet, sunset on the horizon. I mattered to Him. He wanted to take the time to just be with me, to see deep into me, to know me.

That day, He had said to me, "I have been waiting all eternity for this moment."

"What do You want me to know about that memory?" I ask, curiously.

Understanding begins to come. I see that in that moment on the beach, a space in my soul had expanded. I had begun to have a "self" that believes she is indeed worth loving, worth protecting, and worth being seen.

Thoughts come to me. It feels like Jesus explaining. "When you don't have a strong sense of who you are inside, then you need others outside of you to tell you who you are. But others outside of you will not always say, 'You are worth protecting, loving, being seen, and having your needs met.' Sometimes, My love, their actions will say the opposite of that, and what do you do then?"

I do not know. That is what has happened to me. It feels like my husband, my soul-mate, has just said that my needs do not matter, that I am not worth protecting. I am undone. Apparently, my sense of self is not strong enough to endure that level of invalidation.

I sense my Lover, Jesus, say to me, "I am growing this 'soul space' within you to be able to still feel loved, seen, protected, and worth having your needs met, even when those closest to you say otherwise. It will be an inner strength that you have yet to tap into."

That is my joy set before me. This pain I am suffering has a purpose. There is joy on the other side. I will feel secure, safe, and valued in ways I do not yet know. This is what I need in order to live this process well. I will stay in the pain and let it do its work.

Knowing this, I look after my own needs and desires in the process of validating my husband's. I say "yes" to him working part-time for now. That will be somewhat of a sacrifice, but it will mostly affect his time, not mine. But in five weeks when they ask him to go on full time, I will ask him to step down or renegotiate. I want to be faithful to my process and my sabbatical time and not run into the next phase too quickly.

September 5, 2015 – Tapping into Trauma, hijacked by emotion

I am not well. Twenty minutes of a fit of anger has morphed into hopeless despair, and for the first time since I was 15 years old, I want to self-harm. I can feel my arms craving a blade.

Immediately, I realize something is NOT RIGHT with my brain, and the inner dialogue begins.

"You have never cut before! What are you thinking and why?" I hear one part of me say.

"I just want the pain to stop. I want him to realize how much pain I am in right now," another voice opinionates referring to my husband.

Matt just announced that he will be starting the job three days earlier than I thought we had agreed to. I know this is nothing really. It does not merit this fit of rage and hopeless despair. Yes, I feel lied to and robbed from, but that is no cause for this level of emotion. What is going on inside of me? I feel unprotected again, like I sensed on the tram in Gatlinburg, but I see no memories associated with the pain.

The painful thoughts continue, "Jesus died just once for all… and yet I feel like I die every day. No, actually, I feel robbed from and betrayed. It is one thing to willingly give my time, affection, and attention, but when someone just takes it without asking, against my will, it is a different story. And I am SICK of dying over and over again. Maybe I could physically die just once, and it will be all over."

There is a part of me still present enough to know that I am not thinking well. "You are in a ton of pain, Toni," I hear in my mind. "You are stuck in complex emotions and you need help. I think you are actually in a traumatic memory right now, and you don't realize it. You need help. Get up off the floor, go journal, and talk with your husband."

I obey the voice and get a journal and here I am writing. As I share with Matt what is happening to me, I sense compassion from him. He agrees that I probably need to call the trauma therapist.

I call and make an appointment. I am so thankful we have this resource here. I would never be able to get this kind of help in Uruguay. I feel calmed now, but that was very scary. I can't wait to process this. I do not want this happening again.

CHAPTER 29

For Personal Reflection and Practice

As you can see, it is very important for me to notice when I am feeling *more* than the situation merits. This is how I realize my brain is being hijacked by something from my past. I do *not* have to live with this threatening to break into my present at any moment. Thankfully there are wonderful resources to help get to the core issues and find healing. It takes time and energy, but nothing compared to the drain and pain of being thrown back into the past to relive some other trauma that is not even present currently.

If you struggle with similar situations, please find professional help either from Theophostic Prayer Ministry (www.theophostic.com), the Immanuel Approach (www.immanuelapproach.com), or Comprehensive Resource Model (www.comprehensiveresourcemodel.com).

1. Quiet yourself.

2. Go to an interactive appreciation memory.

3. Ask God if there is anything He wants you to know about your past traumas.

Not Alone

September 24, 2015 – Safe Space

I close my eyes as the Comprehensive Resource Model therapist invites me to find my "sacred place," anywhere I feel happy, joyful, or safe.

Within seconds, I am in a field of yellow flowers. It is a large, meadow-like clearing with a dark, deep green forest towering around the edges. I feel like an 8-year-old, safe and playful. And He is here. I love the flowers, and His presence is assuring.

This is a place I used to come to in my mind when I was younger. I am surprised that it surfaces. For the last 10 years, my sacred place has been the beach. But now, back in Tennessee, a younger part of me is beckoning me to come to the safe place of my past.

I come here willingly. I look all around and notice Jesus off to my right just behind me. He is enjoying me as I enter into the moment. I am drawn to the beautiful yellow flowers growing wild all around me. Admiring them, I start to pick a few to make a bouquet, but I sense something… in the forest. It is wolves. I glance at Jesus, and I am flooded with emotion. Am I afraid? I would imagine it would be fear that would well up inside of me, but after a minute, I realize I am not afraid. I am sad. The familiar heaviness of grief takes over my body. I cannot even move my arms. Like lead, it moves through my blood stream and finally finds its way out through my eyes.

He pulls me close. "I know. It *is* sad that they are there. It is sad that there is always danger. We can be sad together." I feel seen and validated. I am not wrong to be sad. I let my tears flow.

"But," He continues, "it is okay here. You are safe. They won't come into the light."

As this truth sinks into my soul, the sadness inside actually grows. "There are people out there who have no safe place to go," I begin explaining, as if He does not already know this. "There are people out there in the woods. There are people being eaten by the wolves." I become almost hysterical. "My 15-year-old daughter is out there."

He holds me close, comforting me. Then, He takes my hand and leads me through the field to a butterfly – no, to a kaleidoscope of butterflies! I had not seen them here before, but they are everywhere. Lightness comes over me. Distracted from my sadness, I enjoy their beauty.

"You don't have to feel sadness for others right now," He whispers into my ear. "This time is for YOU."

I breathe deeply and relax. I surrender to His invitation. Empathy, while it is a strength of mine, can also be one of my greatest weaknesses. I let go of others for now, and I settle into the safety my Creator has made for me.

We walk along playfully and finally toss ourselves to the ground and look up at the sky. The flowers form a bed-like barrier between the hard soil and me. We are hidden in three-feet tall flowers all around us, lying on our backs, hands intertwined with the sky above.

I am safe and sound. I look straight ahead at the clouds. The sky is deep blue and breathtaking. Then clouds come passing by, and as I gaze, I notice all of my intimate memories with Jesus being played like a movie in the sky. I feel His hand holding mine. He is so happy to be with me, and to be remembering with me all of the amazing moments when He has intervened in my pain and brought me back to joy. We enjoy them together, glancing at each other during the good parts.

I feel seen, loved, protected, comforted, and cared for.

We end our session for the day, but I know something significant has just happened. I give thanks again for Jesus' amazing way of joining me, enjoying me right where I am, and giving me the resilience to move on.

September 25, 2015 – I am Not Alone

We called 911 for our oldest daughter last night. She was triggered after therapy, and the pain was too much for her to handle. How do *I* cope through all of this? I know it always gets worse before it gets better. I just want to be stable for her during her ups and downs. "How do I do it, Papa?"

I feel led to go outside to the trampoline. I follow my intuition without question. I have learned from Godly Play that sometimes our body knows what we need, even if we do not have words for it. I lie down on my back, look up at the clouds, and thaw to worship music. The sky is gorgeous, the weather perfect, just like in my imagination the day before in my safe place.

The songs "I am not Alone," "Forever," and "Ocean's Deep" accompany me as I let grief and fear fill my body, soul, and mind. I feel Him with me, too, just like He was in the field of flowers. I glance over my shoulder and put out my hand to take His. We make eye contact. I truly am NOT alone. The fear disappears as I look in His eyes.

Pain floods. Gratitude and grief, hand in hand. I look away, up to the clouds. We watch them again as they play our memories, our moments. I rest. I pray for my precious daughter.

After an hour or so of this, I sense in my imagination Jesus leading me into the forest where the wolves are. Allie, my daughter, is out there in the woods. She is exposed. Jesus carries light with us; it emanates from His very body. He *is* the light. As long as I stay with Him, in His light, I am safe.

He stops, turns to me and surprisingly names me again, "You are Toni, My precious restorer. You will restore to Me those who are broken."

"Is this even true?" I ask myself, wondering if I am just making all of this up in my own head.

"Believe what you see," I hear.

I see me putting people's hands into the hands of Jesus. I see myself helping equip pastors, therapists, and counselors to better deal with trauma and mental illness. Then I see my Allie and wonder if she will ever be restored. Will her hands ever reach for His?

"What do you see?" He asks.

I look into the future, and I see her with Jesus, laughing, enjoying, being enjoyed.

"Believe what you see," I hear again.

"But I am scared I will mess it up, say the wrong thing, or not share more of the right thing at the right time."

"Do you think I am limited by how you respond to her?" He lovingly laughs at the absurdity of that thought.

I join His laughter, recognizing how preposterous the idea sounds.

"I am so much bigger than all of that," He continues. "Trust Me. Follow Me. Listen to Me. Rest in Me."

"Trust Me." Some of the very first words I ever sensed my Lord saying to me. I am stayed. I am calmed. I am with Him, and He is everything. I am Toni Maria, precious sea of sorrow and strength. I am a restorer. And I must know my limits. He is The Restorer. I am simply the messenger delivering the message of reconciliation, putting one's hand into the hand of Jesus.

I come back to the present, to the clouds in the sky. I cannot help but smile. And the words "I am not alone" resound in my mind, in my body, and in my soul.

CHAPTER 30

For Personal Reflection and Practice

1. Do you have an imaginative, safe place or a sacred place where you can go when life gets rough? It could be based on a real place, but it could also be something you have made up. Close your eyes, breathe deeply, and ask yourself where you feel the safest, or what place you feel is most sacred (set apart) to you. Spend some time there exploring. What do you see, hear, smell? Who is there with you? How do you feel when you go there in your imagination?

2. The next time you feel overwhelmed, try to take some time alone to go to your safe place and interact with Jesus there. It takes time for our souls to feel all that we need to feel and find a resting place. Do you give yourself that time? Or do you run around avoiding your feelings?

3. I am reminded of Hebrews 4:14-16:
    "[14] Since then we have a great high priest who has passed through the heavens, Jesus, the Son of God, let us hold fast our confession. [15] For we do not have a high priest who is unable to sympathize with our weaknesses, but one who in every respect has been tempted as we are, yet without sin. [16] Let us then with confidence draw near to the throne of grace, that we may receive mercy and find grace to help in time of need."

    What does it look like for you to "draw near to the throne of grace"? What does it look like to "receive mercy and find grace to help in time of need"? Close your eyes and imagine these verses. What do they look like to you? What images come to mind? Write down whatever you sense.

CHAPTER 31

Deeper Still

September 28, 2015 – Little One

We begin today's session by breathing and listening to my body. I notice my arms are heavy. It is the same heaviness that comes when I am sad, like lead through my blood.

I am also angry. I have several memories popping through my mind, and I realize I am angry because often, when I was a child, my dad did not make things fair. At times, he was unpredictable and precarious, parenting for himself instead of what was best for us. I could feel the anger rising, but as always, it turns to tears.

I don't know why these memories are surfacing again. I have processed these already! I let go of trying to understand or control the work of healing in my life. I let myself feel all that is surfacing about my childhood.

Within a few minutes, I am feeling the same way I had felt in the episodes of intense emotion a few weeks back. I am rocking and crying, the physical pain surfacing full on.

Then, the memory comes. "I am 3 or 4 years old," I begin to tell the therapist. "I do not know the details of what happened except that I was pitching a fit over something. I have no idea what. But what I do remember is that it ends with me lying on the floor in the hallway all-alone, crying and screaming until I eventually fall asleep. I had clearly been in distress."

That is where my pain is coming from. I begin to cry, "She needed someone to see her and help her understand what was happening to her. She needed to know why she felt things so strongly, and that no matter how she felt, someone was glad to be with her."

I want to go to her, to be this parent for her. So I do. I show up in the memory and kneel down to where she is on the floor. Touching my hand to her face, I gently invite her glance. She is so cute, so precious. She timidly looks at me, face still red from screaming and crying.

"You are not alone, Little One, I am here," I say to her, and she quickly crawls into my arms and leaves the floor.

Time disappears and cosmic internal shifts are happening in me deep within where words do not exist.

"I am here. You are so sad and angry. But it is okay. Look, Jesus is here, too."

I could feel Him over my shoulder, tenderly present, protecting, approving, enjoying what He was witnessing.

The Little One is relieved. She nuzzles into me and releases her emotions to me. She is feeling rescued and safe. She has been on that floor alone in her pain for 38 years now. As I hold her, I can feel the relief flood into my soul. I heave her tears and try to remember to breathe.

Simultaneously, I am grieved that it has taken so long to come for her. I have had this memory all of my life and yet never knew what to do about it. Never knew it was so important.

We communicate without words. Memories of the last few weeks flood my mind, and I realize what she has been trying to help me understand.

"When I was in a fit of rage a few weeks back, was that you?" I ask. Her little head sheepishly nods up and down.

"And when I was stuck in anger and hopeless despair and thought about cutting, was that you?" She looks at me in grief and confirms my wonderings.

"I was trying to get you to come. It was the only way I knew how," she says, and another wave of tears comes over me.

"Well, you did a good job, and I am here," I say, relieved that I have been brought to the source of that terrifying fit I had in the bathroom a few weeks back. "You never have to be alone again. You have me, and we have Jesus. All of your emotions are safe with me. I am glad to be with you even when you are sad, mad, angry, hopeless, or all of the above. We can handle them together because we can feel Jesus' presence with us through them all."

It feels like I am introducing this child state of mine to Jesus for the first time. I want to tell her how precious she is to Him. I glance at Jesus to see if that is okay, and He smiles and nods to go ahead.

"Little Toni, you are the precious beloved one." She opens her eyes big, and we are transported to every memory she holds. In each one, I repeat the words to her, "You are precious! You are precious!" She is giddy and joyful. My toes begin to wiggle.

Then something else happens that amazes me: good memories come forth, memories of being enjoyed, of being seen as precious, memories of my parents holding me, caring for me, memories of playing soft ball with my sister's team and being the "adorable mascot." Not new memories, but new in how I am feeling them. I can actually FEEL appreciated, cared for, and loved.

I have wondered for so long why I could not feel the love that was around me. I have wondered what was holding me back. I see now that when I encounter a painful moment that I am not able to feel, I block it as best as I can. But in blocking that painful memory, I also unknowingly numb the good feelings that come with the joy-filled ones as well.

I am left undone and exhausted, but Little One is still sharing with me. It is interesting to me that she shares in memories instead of words, and I am left to guess the meaning.

Memories come like snapshots: the quiet moments when I was 5 staring at God's creation while sitting in my windowsill, dancing alone in my room at 6, joyfully enjoying painting at 10, and playfully writing poetry at 12. This was her. She is telling me that she is the one in me that wants, and needs, a creative outlet. She thrives when she is writing, playing, reflecting, being. I laugh out-loud as it all starts to make sense now.

For years, that part of me had been dormant. The rigorous life of studying and working full time and trying to achieve something in this world had snuffed out these gifts. It wasn't until I was 26 years old that this journey began, and I started re-learning how to listen to my own soul and God's heart again through silence, solitude, and simplicity. It has been 17 years of process that has finally lead to rescuing her off of the floor.

It was her, all along, longing to connect with creativity, with God. It was her limiting my energy levels, making me tired so that I would stop the madness and learn to receive.

"Thank you," I say to her, still holding her in my arms on the floor. "I hated my limitations for years, thought them weakness. Eventually, Jesus has helped me accept my limitations, and live from rest. But I had no idea it was you, Little One, trying to teach me to receive. Thank you.

"Can you trust me to care for you? To listen to you? To protect you?" I ask her.

"Yes," she replies. "You are a great mommy." I feel so touched that she would think so. As she says this, she stands up, steps into my body, and stretches.

That takes me off guard, and I begin to sob again.

"Thank you so much for helping me become a great mommy!" I say to her, to me, the little me inside.

We nestle into Jesus together, and the truth settles into our very soul: "You are not alone. I am not alone. We are not alone."

CHAPTER 31

For Personal Reflection and Practice

Sometimes I just want my pain to go away. Unfortunately, instead of wanting to grow from it, learn from it, or let it have its work in me, I would like to just escape it, numb it, or deny it. This has never proven helpful, however, and usually damages my relationships.

1. What do you characteristically do with your pain?

2. In what ways is that helpful and in what ways it is damaging to you, others or your relationships?

3. How would you like to begin responding to the grief, fear, anxiety, and anger in your life?

4. What resources do you need in order to learn how to respond differently to your pain?

CHAPTER 32

True-Self Space

October 22, 2015 – Done

"I'm done! I am done!" This is all I can hear in my head. I feel robbed of my energy and time. Between my husband and my daughter, I am so exhausted and angry that I honestly don't know how to get out of this. My husband is working instead of living in our sabbatical. He has left no time for our counseling sessions, no time for dealing with undone work from last year, no time for talking about issues with the kids, no time left for us as a couple. He has not only abandoned me, he has abandoned himself.

I am bitter, angry, and done. I have worked on myself and worked on myself. I have tried to explain to him how much it hurts me to see him shut down emotionally. But he doesn't get it. He is totally unable to see *me* right now. He even thinks I am the problem!

I hear in my mind, "He will never understand. He can't. And I am done trying to help him." I feel a strong response coming over me, an extreme response, and it scares me. Twenty-one years of marriage and this is what it has come to?

In shambles, I walk into my therapist's office already at the brink of tears. I am so thankful that I have her to sit with me and help sort out what is going on. I didn't think I would survive long enough to get here.

"Where do you feel connected to your body?" she asks. I am used to this question by now.

In my imagination, I map out points in my body that feel most connected with my emotions. My nervous system is fried. I have been so upset today that I am shaking all over, and I notice that my body cannot even regulate its own temperature. I feel tingly in my arms. My core is sucking energy and heat from the rest of my body. My eyes are tired from crying, my stomach slightly nauseous, and my feet are cold.

"Do you want the system open or closed?" the therapist inquires.

I never really know what she means when she asks that question, but today I respond quickly and definitively, "Closed!" My thoughts are sure and resolved: "I don't want him to touch me anymore," I hear in my mind. "I don't want anyone to touch me!"

I connect my feet to my arms to close the circuit in my imagination. I am a ball suspended in black nothingness, and it feels good. No person or thing can touch me. I want to be alone. I want to be safe.

Memories come: times when I was a teenager and needed my husband, who was then my boyfriend, and he was there… times when I needed him emotionally and he was not there.

Feelings emerge and thoughts follow. "I don't want to depend on him anymore." I manage some words to describe all that is whirling around inside.

"What do you mean?" the therapist probes.

"My soul senses a hint of unhealthy dependence on him. I think I am hitting another threshold of differentiation or individuation, where I need to become more separate so that I can become more interconnected to him, instead of dependent on him. I want to be healthy. I think what is wrong is that I still need him to validate me. I still need him to see me and understand my emotions in order for me to feel valid and important."

My mind brings up other moments when I have struggled. Anytime I am in real need and my loved ones don't acknowledge my need or validate it, I am ripped to shreds.

I hear the words, "You are not worth their time. You are not important."

I spiral inward, expending all of my energy trying to convince some part of me that I AM important, even though others may not be affirming that. But I am tired. I am out of energy. I am done. I know the answer is not to run and isolate myself from the entire world, but to face this head on.

"I know that is the lie." I finally come out of my head to state it out loud, "I AM NOTHING! I AM UNIMPORTANT! I AM NOT WORTH THE TIME!"

I have visited this lie before. I have faced it before. My mind searches the files... I am 9 or 10 years old, my sister closes the door in my face and tells me to leave her alone. I am all ages, watching my dad as he watches TV. I feel invisible to him. I am unseen. I am not important. I see images of him telling me to "stop crying or I'll give you something to cry about!" or "you don't really like that" or "you can't really believe that."

I am slightly frustrated because I am here again. But there must be something new, something I have not seen. "Jesus help!"

And it hits me. "I am not even allowed to feel or think for myself. There is no space for me to wholly exist. No space where I can have my own identity that is distinct, unique, and valid.

Even as I relive these memories, I know this was not the totality of my experience, but it is the only part I am feeling at this moment.

My mind moves on and I am 15 and have learned in church that I am important as long as I am helping others.

This is so sick. Jesus, I am so sick. I have done so much work over the years to overcome this lie, to learn to rest in my relationship with You, to learn to care for myself well, to learn to

275

feel Your delight in me! I have experienced time and time again my Creator and Lover coming to me to show me how important I am, how much You love me, even when I am incapable of doing anything. I feel like I have learned to rest in You and let You enjoy me. And yet, here I am again, facing this lie at another level of my soul.

I see the different parts of me. One part feels very much like a teenager. She is the voice that has been strong today. I imagine her in my mind standing with her arms folded, resolved to protect me at all cost, resolved to be "done with it." She is tired of the pain.

I know she is trying to help me, but her extreme responses will do more harm than good.

Then the more adult side of me speaks, the side that has experienced Jesus over and over again, "What do you need from me? You are taking over and reacting in an extreme way. I see that you are hurting, but we have to work together somehow. I want to work together. What do you need from me?"

Nothing. I get nothing. I am at a loss for how to integrate these two emotional states.

"Ask Jesus," I hear someone suggest in my mind. I almost laugh. "Oh, yes," I say out loud to the therapist, "that is what it is like me to do when I don't know the way forward. Ask Jesus."

"Jesus, where are You in all of this? What do I need to know?"

Slowly, words form in my mind that begin a shift in the innermost region of my soul. "Even the darkness is light to me. I am the darkness that surrounds you, My child."

I can feel my body changing as the words flow through my blood. "I am the darkness and you are suspended in Me."

I see the image of me from the beginning, a ball floating in darkness, but the darkness is not an impersonal void. It is the Spirit of God Himself. The image zooms out and I see Him, my Creator, holding me gently, purposefully, cupping His hands together to form a space... all for me.

He is even respecting that space by not touching me, but

giving me a place to be all alone, and yet held and protected. He is happy to do so. He is eager to do so. He is validating my very existence.

The truth sinks into my mind, body, emotions, and soul: I have a place to wholly exist. I am so important that the very God of the universe is creating, respecting, and protecting this space. I feel validated at the deepest level of my existence. I feel seen. I feel held, safe, and important. I matter. I really do matter.

I have a "self space," a space for my *true* self to be. God values me! He is paying attention to me! I can see Him there in my imagination looking on, holding me. I have my own identity from God that is enjoyable, unique, and beautiful. I matter. This is my "self space," or should I say my "*true*-self space." It is a space dependent on no one else but God. A space God Himself created and is validating, ordaining, and blessing. It is good.

My body relaxes completely. My temperature is regulating itself again, my heart rate is normal, my nervous system at rest. I am in complete peace: physically, emotionally, and spiritually.

I try to return to the previous feelings of "unimportant," the bitter, angry, all-done place. I try to see if there is any remnant of these feelings left.

Nothing. Just peace.

I feel like Neo in the Matrix when he resurrects from the dead. The enemies begin unloading their bullets on him, but he calmly says, "no", and begins to take over the program that has kept humans enslaved for generations. He holds up his hand, stops the bullets in mid air, and curiously takes one in his fingers and examines it. As they fall to the floor he realizes he is completely free from their control. I am completely free from feeling unimportant based on how someone treats me, or what they think of me. I curiously examine the bullets that have come at me, and they fall to the ground.

Jesus' words from a few days ago come to mind, "I am growing this 'soul space' within you to be able to still feel loved, seen, protected, and worth having your needs met, even when those closest to you say otherwise. It will be an inner strength that you have yet to tap into."

I am effortlessly tapping into this strength. It is amazing.

"Well, how do you feel about your husband ignoring and invalidating your feelings and perspective?" the therapist probes.

"It's not about me." The thought forms from deep within, a knowing, not me trying to convince my inner self, but coming *from* my inner self, from the place where I sense God's light-darkness all around me. It is a space that holds my *true* self, the person I was created to be.

"When others do things that communicate that I am not important, it is *not* even about *me*. It is about them, their fear, their anger, their insecurity, their pain, their stuck places. It is not about me."

Then this truth begins to infiltrate every memory from my past. In my imagination, I see my "*true*-self space" popping around like a honeybee pollinating a dozen flowers. It lands in the memory, shares the truth, and creates new meaning for me, all of me, every age of me, every stage of me.

I don't need my loved ones to validate my needs in order for them to be worth meeting. I don't need them to understand or "get it." I understand. I get it. My perspective is valid and worth listening to because I am valid and worth listening to. God has ordained it so, and it is so.

I can ask for what I need without anger or ultimatums, without manipulation or guilt.

I am marveling at this new reality. I sense in my mind satisfaction coming from my teenage-self. She has done her work. She has protected me, but now, she no longer has to because I know how valuable I am, how important I am. I can now live out of this truth without needing her extreme responses. I smile, and I thank her. She nods trustingly. We will live out of our true-self, the one God has created for us. We will live in His pleasure and His delight. Thank You, Father, for going deeper still in order to bring me back to joy.

I can sense that this experience has made a quantum shift in my soul. I leave a different woman. I have broken the cocoon and can fly free into my marriage, my family, and my vocation a more mature woman, a woman who knows to the core of her soul who she is and whose she is.

CHAPTER 32

For Personal Reflection and Practice

Differentiation has been an important concept for me to understand. Developed by Murray Bowen, the founder of modern family systems theory, it refers to my ability to hold on to all I know to be true about myself regardless of the opinions of others. It is my ability to let others be who they are, while still being able to follow my life goals that are determined from within and still remain close to those important to me.

I know I am well differentiated when...

- I can express myself and my needs/wants in an invitational way without putting others down or needing others to do what I want them to do.
- I can work interdependently with those around me because I am not afraid they will consume me, control me, or abuse me. I can take responsibility for my own life.
- I can offer non-anxious leadership in the midst of crisis.
- I can respect differing opinions without needing to convince them or change them to my opinion.
- I can feel peace no matter what those around me are feeling.
- I can see the other person's process as separate from mine and validate it and support it, even if I don't agree with how they are going about it.
- I can live from my *true* self, the self that God has created, validated, named and called forth, unaffected by criticism or praise.
- I can rest, play and enjoy those around me.

(see Peter Scazzero's *Emotionally Healthy Spirituality* for a great discussion on differentiation)

1. Which of these characteristics do you feel like you do well?

2. Which of these characteristics do you feel like you need to work on?

3. Breathe deeply, go to an interactive appreciation memory, and ask Jesus what He wants you to know about how well you are able live from your *true* self when in relationship with others who might not approve. What do you need most from Him right now?

A Word After

March 2016

These experiences have changed how I am in every relationship I currently have, from my marriage to my vocation. There is a solid "me" from which I live, love, and work. For the last four months, I have not exhausted myself with self-doubt and fear. I am able to center more quickly and sense my "*true*-self space" hidden in Christ, which allows me to feel all that I need to feel and respond in a healthier, more compassionate way to the situations around me.

I do not respond perfectly at all, but I am freer to see the other in my responses.

Almost every day after waking up, I stay in bed for at least 15 extra minutes in order to sense Jesus with me and begin my day feeling loved and cared for. My mind browses our joy-moments together, and I feel Him beside me, snuggling me into His body, safe and warm.

I purposefully stay in bed because I want to physically remind myself that my work begins with rest, that He is already working, and that the first part of my work is to sense Him with me, feel His delight in me, listen, and only then follow Him into the great adventure the day will bring!

This does not mean that I have all the energy in the world, or that I never feel sad. On the contrary, this practice allows me to get in touch with what I *do* feel and share it with my Creator. Sadness is actually part of my daily experience because gratitude, unfortunately, has a way of bringing grief with it. This world is oh, so broken, and sadness is an appropriate response to the pain of loss all around me. Feeling my sadness and sensing God's perspective physically and emotionally lightens my load and helps me go into my day grounded and compassionate.

This also does not mean that I never feel overwhelmed. That would be an unrealistic expectation! I used to live trying to avoid feeling that way, because I hated the desperate feelings of shame that would come with it. But now, I no longer have to fear being overwhelmed or try to prevent it, because I can sense how enjoyed I am even in the middle of it. I can let it wash over me like a wave, knowing that even if it tears me to pieces, my Lover and Creator will heal me and put me back together again.

I do not know where you are on your journey towards emotional health and maturity. I do not know how hard or easy it might be for you to manage your emotions and your relationships with all of those around you. I do not know what you do with your pain or the pain of those with whom you have relationship.

But I do know that we have a Creator, Immanuel, God with us, who is here longing to be your source of "glad to be with you no matter what!" He longs to remove whatever is hindering you from being all that He has created you to be. He longs to comfort you, have compassion on you, heal you, and make you whole. His Spirit is closer than your breath and can be heard inside your very own thoughts.

If you so choose to follow Him back to joy, remember God approaches each of us with complete individuality. How you experience Him will be entirely different based on who you are – male/female, younger/older, extravert/introvert, etc. We have all been given different materials to work with and cannot compare our experiences with others. But, we can long for intimacy and learn to pay attention to all that goes on inside of us and around us as we seek to listen.

What is Jesus saying to you about what you have read? What are your next steps? Who will you journey with? The story is yours to be lived. May it be filled with deep satisfaction as you, too, follow your way back to joy.

If this book has touched your life, and you would like to spread the joy,
go to
www.amzn.to/1XGuL9x
and leave a review for others to see

Can you imagine a self-propagating movement of joy, where families are glad to be together, churches are no longer shame based, our workplaces and schools are thriving and hope is abundant?

That is why I have shared my story through this book, and why I am already working on a book on parenting back to joy.

Believe it or not, one small way you can be a part of igniting the joy revolution is by reviewing this book on Amazon and spreading the word to others.

Thanks so much for joining me!

Appendix: Helpful Resources

These are the resources that have been most helpful to me on my back-to-joy journey.

Helpful Books

Boundaries: When to Say Yes, How to Say No to Take Control of Your Life by Henry Cloud and John Townsend

The Complete Guide to Living with Men by E. James Wilder

Daring Greatly: How the Courage to Be Vulnerable Transforms the Way We Live, Love, Parent, and Lead by Brené Brown

Fighting for Your Marriage: A Deluxe Revised Edition of the Classic Best-seller for Enhancing Marriage and Preventing Divorce by Howard J. Markman and Scott M. Stanley

The Gifts of Imperfection: Let Go of Who You Think You Are Supposed to Be, and Embrace Who You Are by Brené Brown

Healing Life's Hurts: Through Theophostic Prayer by Dr. Ed Smith

Hearing God: Developing a Conversational Relationship with God by Dallas Willard

Joy Starts Here: The Transformation Zone by E. James Wilder, Edward M. Khouri, Chris M. Coursey, Shelia D. Sutton

Joyful Journey: Listening to Immanuel by E. James Wilder, Anna Kang, John Loppnow, Sungshim Loppnow

Living from the Heart Jesus Gave You by E. James Wilder (Author), James G. Friesen (Contributor), Anne M. Bierling (Contributor), Rick Koepcke (Contributor), Maribeth Poole (Contributor)

Mindsight: The New Science of Personal Transformation by Dr. Daniel J. Siegel

Outsmarting Yourself: Catching Your Past Invading the Present and What to Do about it by Dr. Karl Lehman

Parenting With Love and Logic by Foster Cline and Jim Fay

Rising Strong: The Reckoning, the Rumble, the Revolution by Brené Brown

The Spirit of the Disciplines: Understanding How God Changes Lives by Dallas Willard

Helpful Websites

Life Model Works/Joy Starts Here: www.joystartshere.com

On this site, you will find everything you need in order to grow joy, resilience, and relational skills for you, your family, and the environments in which you work and study. I highly recommend the Connexus courses (www.joystartshere.com/connexus), as well as the Thrive Leadership Training (www.joystartshere.com/thrivetraining) for those who are leading communities.

Immanuel Approach: www.immanuelapproach.com

Dr. Karl Lehman has put together this website to provide resources for anyone wanting to learn about, receive, facilitate, or teach the Immanuel approach (also known as Emmanuel prayer). This is where you will understand more about letting Jesus lead you to your past to heal wounds and speak His truth. He also has very helpful articles explaining the differences and similarities between Theophostic and Immanuel Prayer, as well as Theophostic and other secular trauma recovery models.

Lk10 Communities: www.lk10.com

On this site, you will find everything you need from becoming a vibrant family of Jesus to training others in how to pastor their families and communities. "Church" is made very practical and simple. There are courses to take as well as opportunities to engage with a coach. If you are looking for how to live out emotionally healthy spirituality in community, starting with your own family, this is the place to begin.

Theophostic Prayer Ministry: www.theophostic.com

Theophostic Prayer is "intentional and focused prayer with the desired outcome of an authentic encounter with the presence of Christ, resulting in mind renewal and subsequent transformed life." This website is a great way to get to know about this prayer ministry. They are currently revamping everything and will soon offer all of their training for FREE!

SELF-PUBLISHING
SCHOOL

NOW IT'S YOUR TURN

Discover the EXACT 3-step blueprint you need to become
a bestselling author in 3 months.

Self-Publishing School helped me, and now I want them to help
you with this FREE VIDEO SERIES!

Even if you're busy, bad at writing, or don't know where to start,
you CAN write a bestseller and build your best life.

With tools and experience across a variety niches and professions,
Self-Publishing School is the <u>only</u> resource you need to
take your book to the finish line!

DON'T WAIT

Watch this FREE VIDEO SERIES now, and
Say "YES" to becoming a bestseller:

https://xe172.isrefer.com/go/curcust/Tonimdaniels

Made in the USA
Columbia, SC
11 December 2019

84681892R00174